MULAN

DISNEY MULAN

Adapted by Elizabeth Rudnick

Screenplay by Rick Jaffa & Amanda Silver

and Lauren Hynek & Elizabeth Martin

Based on Disney's *Mulan*

Disney Mulan: Book of the Film
A CENTUM BOOK 978-1-913265-29-8
Published in Great Britain by Centum Books Ltd
This edition published 2020
1 3 5 7 9 10 8 6 4 2

Centum Books Ltd, 20 Devon Square,
Newton Abbot, Devon, TQ12 2HR, UK

books@centumbooksltd.co.uk

CENTUM BOOKS Limited Reg. No. 07641486

A CIP catalogue record for this book is available from the British Library

Printed in the United Kingdom.

DISNEY

MULAN

ONE

The morning sun had long since risen over the Chinese tulou that Mulan called home. As she stood in the middle of the circular compound of connected buildings that was made up of her home and those of her neighbors, she was surrounded by the muffled sounds of the nearby villagers. From a second-floor balcony a mother called to her daughter to bring the laundry. In a kitchen on the ground floor, a spoon banged against the sides of a pot as another mother prepared the evening meal. From the opening between the buildings that led to the street, Mulan could make out the low moos of several large cows being herded to a new feeding ground and the occasional squawk as their heavy feet plodded precariously close to a stray chicken. Coming from her own home, nestled in the middle of all the others, Mulan heard the steady *click, click, clack, clack* of the shuttle as her mother and younger sister wove fabric.

But the sounds did nothing to distract Mulan. She had grown up with them. She had spent every day of her seven years next to the same handful of villagers. At present, the clangs and bangs were merely background noise to her current mission: herding the chickens to their coop.

Unfortunately, the chickens were not in the mood to be herded. For the past hour, Mulan and her father, Hua Zhou, had been trying to move the small group of feathered animals from one side of the courtyard to the other. Yet each time they got most of the birds going in the same direction, one would break off and make a run for it. Sweat dotted Mulan's forehead from running back and forth in front of her father as she tried to stop the chickens. Her arm was beginning to ache from hitting her wooden stick on the ground to get the birds' attention. Still, there was a bounce to her step, and while her father seemed ready for the task to be over, Mulan was eager to continue. She loved a challenge. And chicken herding was certainly that.

"Steady, Mulan . . ."

Her father's voice was stern, but kind. Looking up, she saw Zhou's warm brown eyes looking down at her. She met his smile. She knew that many people in her village were intimidated by her father. He always walked with his head high, his chest out. Once a fierce warrior, his body had grown more fragile with age. His shoulders stooped ever so slightly and his hair was no longer thick. Yet he still had an air of confidence despite the limp that forced him to walk with a cane. But to Mulan, he was not fierce or scary. He was her father. And she adored him.

At seven years old, Mulan knew she was supposed to spend her time helping her mother take care of their home, but she had no interest in weaving or cooking or cleaning. Just the idea of those boring chores was enough to make her yawn. Her little sister, Xiu, loved to do—and excelled at—those tasks. So it was a much better use of her time, Mulan had argued on more than one occasion, for Mulan to help her father, who had no sons to deal with things like pesky chickens, and let Xiu work with her mother.

A loud squawk brought Mulan's thoughts back to her task. As if finally realizing that the coop meant food and rest, the chickens began to move toward it in a group. Mulan let out a happy little whoop, startling an old woman standing inside the shrine that sat in the middle of the communal courtyard. She was lighting incense at the base of the large phoenix statue that dominated the shrine. Like the rest of the compound, the shrine had seen better days. Tiles fell off the roof, and more than a few boards were loose. The statue, however, remained in good shape. To those who lived in the village, the statue was the most sacred and important part of their little world. It was a representation of their ancestors, a connection to those who had come before. Every man, woman, and child spent at least some part of every day in the shrine, enjoying the stillness and peace the place brought. Most of the time.

For one moment, it seemed Mulan's job was complete. As Mulan stood back, her father ushered the last of the birds toward the coop's open door. Out of the corner of her eye, Mulan caught sight of a lone chicken veering from the rest of the group. Mulan frowned. She looked back at her father. Zhou was distracted, making sure each chicken got inside. He didn't notice there was an escapee. A look of determination crossed her face. Quietly, she slipped away, ducking and weaving around a few neighbors as she followed the chicken toward the rough wooden building.

Mulan kept her pace steady and her footsteps slow. In her head she heard her father's voice as he told her, not for the first time, the tale of the turtle and the hare. No one had believed the slow-moving, deliberate turtle could win a race against the speedy hare. Yet while the hare ran himself ragged, the turtle slowly and steadily made his way across the finish line. A part of her knew that she should be like the turtle: wait and allow the chicken to realize it was hungry and go to the coop on its own. But the other part of her—the part that was very, *very* bad at taking things slow and steady and, similar to the hare, liked to sprint to the end—didn't want to wait.

As she watched the chicken move farther out of her reach, Mulan's heart began to pound and her fingers began to twitch. Her pace quickened. First a faster walk, then a slow jog, until she took off in a sprint after the chicken. Hearing Mulan's footsteps, the chicken let out a loud *Bwack!* and ran faster, flapping its wings wildly, sending feathers flying.

The race was on!

Through the courtyard Mulan chased after the chicken. But every time her fingers were nearly close enough to reach out and grab the bird, the pesky animal would duck to the side, gaining freedom for another moment.

Having noticed what his daughter was doing, Zhou shouted, "Mulan! Forget the chicken!" But Mulan's steps didn't slow.

She barely registered the fact that the bird had headed back toward the coop by way of the shrine until she was inside the circular structure. Caught up in the moment, Mulan continued to follow the chicken, which awkwardly flew up and over the phoenix statue. Mulan took a running jump and followed, sailing over the ancient holy relic. Her feet managed to clear it . . . but the stick she was still carrying did not.

With a loud CRACK! the stick slammed into the large stone bird, knocking off its left wing. Outside the shrine, other villagers looked up from their chores at the loud sound, letting out a collective gasp as the wing fell to the ground with a thud. They had paid little mind to Mulan's antics—until now.

Mulan didn't notice. She was already out of the shrine and sprinting behind the chicken up a stairwell to a balcony on the second floor of the building. Catching sight of the charging girl, a young mother, clutching her baby in her arms, jumped out of the way just in time to avoid Mulan's flailing limbs. Racing along, Mulan ducked under a bin of rice held by two men—and right into a woman hanging her laundry. The woman screamed as laundry—and more feathers—went flying.

"Mulan! Take control of yourself!"

At the sound of her mother's voice, Mulan's

footsteps slowed. Ahead, she saw her mother, Li, standing by the door to their home, arms crossed and a frown on her otherwise beautiful face. Beside her was Xiu. Unlike their mother, the expression on Xiu's face was one of delight as she watched Mulan—and the chicken—running toward them along the thin balcony outside their apartment.

Up ahead, the chicken had reached the end of the balcony and once again flew into the air. The creature's short wings and heavy body kept it from going far, but it was able to make it to the rooftop, where it once again took off. Mulan regained her original fast pace and didn't slow, even as the end of the balcony grew closer and closer. At the very last moment, Mulan reached out and grabbed a hanging clothesline. Quickly, she shinnied up it until she, too, made it to the top of the slanted roof.

Mulan came to a sudden stop, her feet balanced on the peak of the roof. In front of her, the lush green countryside spread out to the horizon. Grass on the rolling hills waved in the gentle wind, like waves on the water. Mulan's breath, coming in gasps, hitched. The world was so big, so vibrant. She wished, not for the first time, to go and explore what was beyond the horizon. But there was no way she could ever leave. Her life, her fate, were tied to the very building upon which she stood. And as her mother liked to say, there was no escaping fate.

BWACK!

The chicken's taunting cluck dragged Mulan's thoughts from the impossible back to the present. Narrowing her eyes, she began to move along the roof. Below her, the group of villagers that had been attracted to the courtyard by the sound of the phoenix statue's wing crashing down stared up at Mulan. Horror and disapproval lined their faces. A few of the older women whispered among themselves, not bothering to keep their disappointed tones quiet.

As if it had decided the game was over, the chicken stopped, walked over to the edge of the roof, and with a quick flap of its wings, glided to the ground below. Letting out one last *BWACK* for good measure, it sauntered into the coop.

Watching the chicken, Mulan gave a nod of satisfaction. On the ground below, her father rushed over and slammed the gate shut behind the troublesome bird. She felt a small surge of pride. At least one crisis had been averted.

But as her father's gaze lifted and met hers, Mulan saw there was still one more problem to be solved. She had made it up to the roof, but how was she going to get down? She eyed the distance between where she stood and the spot far below where the chicken had landed. Determination flooded through her, and she clenched her fists at her sides.

"Mulan," her father said, recognizing the look in her eyes, "listen very carefully. You will take a calming breath, and then slowly—*slowly*—you will climb down." Mulan's eyes didn't move from the coop and the offending chicken now safely inside. "*Climb*," he repeated. "Do you understand?"

Mulan did not reply at once. She felt as though time had stopped. The wind had ceased to blow across her cheeks, and all she could hear was the air coming in and out of her lungs and her heart pounding against her chest. Her toes tingled, itching to move. One step and she could jump. One step and she, like the chicken, could *fly*. But then time resumed. Breeze once again fluttered against her face. Shaking her head, she let her gaze drift from the coop, over the gathered crowd and once more to her father.

"Yes," she said.

Zhou started to smile but the smile turned to a gasp as Mulan took a not-so-slow step forward. In her haste, she tripped on the slippery slate roof. Her arms swung out, windmilling wildly at her sides as she struggled to get her balance. But it was too late. She was too off-kilter. As the gathered group below let out a collective gasp, Mulan fell.

For a dreadful moment, Mulan was sure she was plummeting to her death.

But then her mind cleared. The same sensation of time slowing returned and, as if it were highlighted by a ray of sun, a lone beam jutting out from one of the balconies caught Mulan's eye. Contorting her body in a way that seemed to defy gravity, Mulan stopped flailing her arms and reached out a steady hand to grab it. Using the beam, Mulan slowed her descent. Her body stopped falling and instead began to swing like a pendulum around the beam. When she gained enough control, she let go and flipped in the air, landing safely on the ground—and on her feet.

Unhurt, Mulan looked around at the crowd. Her eyes were sparkling, and her cheeks were flushed from the exhilaration and pride she felt for sticking her landing.

And then she looked over at her father. Zhou didn't say anything. He didn't need to. His feelings were written all over his face. What Mulan had just done, the damage she had created and the danger she had put herself in, were too much. Mulan had disappointed him.

The smile on her face disappeared.

TWO

Mulan sat behind Xiu, absentmindedly brushing her sister's long black hair. In front of her, the younger girl was quiet, lost in her thoughts. Mulan didn't mind the silence. Her own brain was loud and busy enough.

All she could see was her father's look of disappointment. It haunted her like a nightmare she couldn't wake from, making her feel shaky and uncomfortable. The last thing she would ever want to do was hurt her father. But she hadn't had a choice. Or at least, that was what she kept telling herself. There was no way her father could have given chase, not with his weak leg. While her father may have been a hero in the war, his injury kept him from working as hard as he would like to in the village. Mulan had simply wanted to help.

And somehow, she seemed to have done just the opposite.

"Mulan?"

Xiu's quiet voice interrupted Mulan's dark thoughts. Her hand stopped, the brush hovering over Xiu's hair as she waited to hear what her sister wanted to say.

"What happened when you fell off the roof?" Xiu asked.

Mulan didn't need to question what Xiu meant. She had felt something . . . odd . . . as she fell through the air. Like somehow her mind had seen a step ahead and her body had known the moves it needed to make before she was even aware herself. But she wasn't about to admit her thoughts out loud—especially to her younger sister. "I was chasing that naughty chicken," she said instead as she resumed combing Xiu's hair.

Beneath the comb, Xiu shook her head. "No,"

she pressed. "When you *slipped*. For a moment it was like you were a bird. . . ." The younger girl's voice trailed off.

Mulan frowned, surprised by her sister's astute observation. Xiu was right. She had felt like a bird. As she had swooped and swung around that beam, she hadn't felt scared. She had felt *alive*. More alive than she had ever felt before. She had been like a bird soaring through the sky, playing on the wind. Not a clumsy chicken but a graceful bird of prey.

But how was that even possible? She hadn't dared think about it until this very moment, but she knew that she had narrowly escaped getting hurt—or worse. Somehow, whatever that *feeling* inside her was, it had managed to save her. Which sounded strange. Which meant there was no way she was going to say it aloud to her sister, because Xiu would *definitely* think it was strange. So instead, Mulan changed the subject.

"Xiu," she said, her hand growing still. "Don't panic. But there's a spider crawling in your hair."

Xiu's shoulders crept up toward her ears and she turned to look at Mulan, worry creasing her innocent face. "You know I'm afraid of spiders," she said, her lower lip beginning to tremble. Then her eyes narrowed. "This isn't one of your tricks, is it Mulan?"

Mulan tried not to smile. "Don't move," she said. "If you hold very still, I will *squash* it. . . ." Her voice trailed off as, from the room below, she heard her mother's voice rise.

"You indulge her," Li said, her loud voice carrying from the living room. Mulan and Xiu paused to listen. Closing her eyes, Mulan held her breath. She could picture her mother and father going through their nightly routine: her mother tidying up while her father slowly unlaced the binding on his leg. Only on this particular night, they were not going about it as quietly as they usually did.

"There's no harm in herding chickens," Zhou retorted.

Mulan heard the soft, even footsteps of her mother as the woman moved closer to her husband. "You know I'm not talking about chickens," she went on. "I'm talking about her . . . her bold spirit. We can't encourage it."

"Mulan is young," Zhou countered. "She's still learning to control herself."

Up in her room, Mulan bristled. She knew her father meant well, but he was talking about her as if she were an untamed filly, not his daughter. She shifted on her seat, wishing she could stop the conversation while at the same time curious to see where it would go. She didn't have to wait long.

"You make excuses for her!" Li said, her voice laced with frustration. "You forget Mulan is a *daughter*, not a son. A daughter brings honor through marriage."

"Any man would be fortunate to marry our Mulan," Zhou said.

Hearing the certainty in her father's voice, Mulan bit her lip. She wanted to be the girl he believed her to be. Maybe chasing that chicken *had* been a little bit reckless. And maybe she *should* have listened to her father when he told her to stop. But did her silly actions now really stand to ruin her marriage options in the future?

As if hearing her daughter's thoughts, Li continued, "Xiu gives me no trouble. The Matchmaker will find a good husband for her." Mulan didn't have to be in the room to imagine the frown on her mother's face or the way she nervously rubbed her temple. When she spoke again, her voice sounded sad, anguished. "It is Mulan I worry about. Always Mulan." There was another pause, and then she continued, her voice almost impossible to hear: "I just don't know where she fits in this world."

The room below grew silent.

Mulan felt her sister's eyes on her but she refused to lift her head. Instead, she stared down at the comb in her lap, rubbing anxiously at the bristles. Her mother's voice echoed in her head. Was her mother right? Was there no place for her in the world? She slowly let out a shaky breath. She had never felt like she truly belonged among the other girls of the village, always the first one to end up in a mud puddle or rip the hem of her shirt. She had always felt more comfortable beside her father in the field than with her mother by the stove. Yet she had never thought that was wrong . . . until now.

"She doesn't mean it," Xiu said.

Mulan stayed silent. She wasn't ready to speak.

But her sister was nothing if not determined. "Tell me about the spider," she pressed.

"There is no spider," Mulan mumbled. She wasn't in the mood for a game.

"How many legs does it have?" Xiu went on, ignoring her sister's grumbles and frown.

Mulan sighed. "You know spiders have eight legs," she answered, unable to stop herself.

"It's not black, is it?" Xiu said, pretending to look frightened, as if a real spider were there and crawling toward her. She waited to see what Mulan would do, or say, next.

Mulan looked at her sister. Xiu's face was still innocent and full of hope, and while Mulan wanted nothing more than to wallow in her own self-pity for a few more moments, she had never been able to say no to Xiu. She was powerless against her sister's huge heart. And so she slowly began to nod. "Yes, it *is* black. With red spots," she said, warming to the idea as she continued. "And I'm sorry to say that it's unusually hairy. And it's crawling toward your *neck* right now!" She reached out her fingers and ran them up and down Xiu's neck.

In response, Xiu shrieked. As Mulan's frown faded completely, she allowed herself a smile. Her mother might not be sure where she fit in the larger world, but right now, Mulan cared more about making her sister laugh and enjoying the moment.

There would be plenty of time to worry about her future—later.

Unfortunately, *later* didn't prove to be later enough. Waking from a terrible nightmare in which she was running from a human-sized chicken, Mulan sat up in her bed, her heart pounding. Outside, beams of moonlight illuminated the night. Mulan got up and walked to the window and looked out into the courtyard below.

In the center, the ancestral shrine stood glowing in white beams of light. A few candles burned weakly, just enough to throw shadows over the phoenix statue—and its missing wing.

Maybe, Mulan thought, *I could fix everything . . . if I fixed the phoenix.*

Tiptoeing out of her room, down the stairs, and into the kitchen, she reached into the cupboard and pulled out a big bowl and grinding stone. Moving to the table, she set them down before filling the bowl with the leftover sticky rice from their evening meal. As quietly as she could, she began to grind the rice. The large grains quickly turned to mush, and soon it had become a thick, sticky paste. Satisfied, Mulan picked up the bowl and moved outside.

As she left the house, a cloud drifted across the moon, casting the courtyard and shrine into sudden darkness. For a moment, Mulan stopped. Perhaps she should just let things be; maybe she had done enough damage as it was. But then the cloud moved, and once more the shrine grew bright. The phoenix, always frozen as if about to rise from the ashes, looked hobbled with only one wing. Mulan nodded to herself. She would fix what she had broken.

Walking inside the shrine, Mulan kneeled on the ground. Then she lifted the broken wing and placed it on her lap. Slowly and carefully, she spread the thick paste on the edge of the wing. When the entire side was coated, she stood and walked over to the statue. Reaching up, she reattached the wing to the body. She stood still, her fingers turning white as she kept pressure between the two points on the bird, hoping to seal the bond. When she was sure it had been long enough, she ever so slowly, finger by finger, took her hands away.

Mulan waited, watching to see if the wing would hold.

Hearing footsteps, Mulan kept her eyes locked on the bird. A moment later, she felt her father step beside her. His eyes went to the bird, too. The pair stood in silence, each lost in their own thoughts.

"Mulan," Zhou finally said. His voice was hushed, but firm. "What happened today, I never want to see happen again." He paused, turning so that he was looking at her. When Mulan didn't meet his eyes, he reached out and put a finger underneath her chin to lift her head. "Do you understand?" he asked.

Taking a deep breath, Mulan nodded. Her father smiled but disappointment lingered in his eyes. Mulan hated to see that. His eyes had ever only been filled with kindness and admiration when he looked down at her. Pulling her head free, unable to bear the look any longer, Mulan turned her gaze back to the phoenix. As she watched, the wing began to slide off.

Mulan's eyes filled with tears as the permanence of what she had done hit her.

Not speaking, Zhou reached up and, with some difficulty, pressed the wing back into place. "Do you know why the Phoenix sits at the right hand of the Emperor?" he asked, not taking his eyes from the bird. Mulan shook her head. "She is his guardian. His protector."

"But I broke her," Mulan whispered.

Zhou nodded. "Ah, but did you know she is half male and half female? She is both beautiful *and* strong." He stopped and once more looked into Mulan's eyes. Only now, the disappointment was gone. "Failure is not fatal, Mulan. This is the lesson of the Phoenix. What matters is that each day you rise up and continue. The Phoenix will watch over you. That's her job. *Your* job is to bring honor to your family. Do you think you can do that?"

Mulan looked at her father. She had never heard the lesson of the Phoenix said in such a way. True, she had been taught that the Phoenix protected the Emperor. But watch over *her*? That was different. If the mythical bird could offer protection, the least Mulan could do was offer a sacrifice to her own family. If that meant following her sister's lead and being her mother's shadow, she would do it. If that meant leaving chickens to race away, she would leave them be. She would do what her father asked of her. She would make her family proud, and she would bring honor to them—no matter what kinds of sacrifices she had to make.

Reaching out, she took her father's hand and they walked back to their home. Behind them, the phoenix's wing once again slid off the bird's stone body.

THREE

As the days passed, Mulan tried, and tried, and *tried* to be the honorable daughter who would make her family proud. She dutifully sat by her mother's side and practiced weaving. She let the occasional chicken wander away even though her feet itched to give chase. When the boys of the village gathered in the courtyard to play, she did her best *not* to kick the wayward ball that stopped in her path.

But despite her best intentions, it was hard to

always be good. Sometimes Mulan couldn't control her impulses. Like when she just *had* to nudge the ball back toward the boys, and it was not entirely her fault that when she did, the kick was harder than she anticipated and the ball happened to hit the poor phoenix statue, knocking off its head. Or when she rode her horse, Black Wind, in from the fields a little too fast and knocked over the neighbor's laundry . . . again.

As the days, and then years, passed, Mulan continued to tamp down reckless urges. She worked on making sure her hair was pulled back in a neat bun—at least when the day started. And she stayed far away from the shrine and the chicken coop . . . for the most part. By the time she turned sixteen, she had grown into her long, lanky limbs and was tall, lithe, and beautiful. But every so often, the little girl who had broken the phoenix statue would appear—eager to do something wild and daring.

Arriving home one afternoon from the countryside, where she had been racing with Black Wind, Mulan hastily jumped off the horse's back and put him in his stall. She could smell dinner and knew that she was late. She groaned. Her mother was not going to be pleased. Quickly, she made her way across the courtyard and into her home.

Her family was sitting at the dinner table. Rushing in, Mulan grabbed a plate and joined them. "Black Wind and I rode alongside two rabbits running side by side," she said, picking a piece of rice out of the bowl. "I think one was a male and one was female. . . ." Her voice trailed off as she realized her family hadn't moved. They were all looking at her, the room silent except for her own voice. "What?" she asked, growing worried. Had she left grass in her hair? Was there mud smeared on her face?

Li nervously wrung her hands. She opened her mouth and then shut it. Mulan's eyes narrowed. This couldn't be good. Her mother was never one to shy from stating what was on her mind. But now she seemed almost . . . scared.

"What is it?" Mulan pressed.

"We have excellent news," Li said, though her voice betrayed her uncertainty. "The Matchmaker has found you an auspicious match."

Mulan's breath caught in her throat. She felt the color drain from her face and reached out a hand to steady herself. *Matchmaker? Auspicious match?*

Those were the words she had been dreading ever since she had turned a marriageable age. For months, she had heard other girls in the village giggling about their own matches and had secretly been thrilled when another day passed with no news from the cranky old woman who made her living setting up the eligible girls of the village. Her dream had been that perhaps no match would *ever* be found. That she could continue to live her life the way it was—free.

Her sister was the one who daydreamed of an auspicious match. Whenever she could, Xiu talked about the joys of being a wife. On any given night she would tell Mulan about the recipes she hoped to cook, the clothes she would weave. Xiu rambled for hours about the ways in which she would live to serve the man who would be her husband. How happy she would make him—and her family. To Mulan, that life seemed confining and devoid of adventure.

Mulan knew it would not bring the honor her family wanted, and she would never admit it out loud, but she did not want to get married. She could stay and help her parents instead, she reasoned.

Perhaps make them proud of her in other ways. Mulan looked to her father, hoping he might say something to put an end to this conversation.

Seeing her daughter's desperate look, Li's expression hardened. "Your father and I have spoken about this," she stated.

Zhou nodded, though he looked sad. "Yes, Mulan. It is decided."

"But—" Mulan started to say.

Her father cut her off with a shake of his head. "It is what's best for our family."

Mulan lifted her head and met her father's gaze. In that moment, Mulan felt time pause and then rewind. She remembered being in the shrine, staring at her father in much the same way she did now. She remembered looking down at the broken wing of the phoenix statue. The Phoenix who, her father said, would protect her. She had to believe that the Phoenix was looking after her now and would continue to look after her, even after her marriage. Phoenix or no Phoenix, Mulan had made a vow to her father that she would bring honor to her family. Even if it meant sacrificing her own happiness.

Taking a deep breath, Mulan nodded. "Yes," she said, her voice soft. "It is best. I will bring honor to us all."

As her mother sighed with relief, Mulan sank down into her chair. While her family resumed their regular table conversation, Mulan was silent, lost in her own thoughts. In one moment, her life and her fate had been decided. She had never felt more miserable.

Far from the tulou, a different fate was being decided.

The desert air was clear. In the sky above, the sun shone brilliantly, causing the walled trading post on the horizon to shimmer as if it were a mirage. One of the few such spots in the vast, sprawling desert steppe, the garrison trading place was bustling. People from all over the world moved in and out, bringing goods to sell or trade. The crowded marketplace was full of the sounds of merchants haggling over colorful silk swaths, carpets, gems, and fruit. A myriad of languages blended together. Occasionally, a translator's voice would rise over the din as he helped a buyer haggle for a better price. Despite the electric feel to the air, order reigned. Officials overseeing the trade marked down transactions, keeping those involved honest.

Sitting astride his large stallion, Böri Khan looked across the steppe at the trading post. Under his light armor, his muscles rippled, his skin covered with a fine layer of dust. Like most of the men around him, his long hair was dark and disheveled. But Böri Khan did not care about his appearance. He and his men had traveled a great distance to get there, and while they might have looked tired and worn, they were anything but.

Böri Khan's dark eyes narrowed as he watched the merchants and traders go about their business, completely exposed and unprotected. Under the Emperor's rule, the people had grown lazy. There had been no wars, nor even the threat of war, in years. People had forgotten the days when the Rourans had run rampant over the Empire, instilling fear with the simple mention of their name. The famed Shadow Warriors had caused trading posts like this one to shut down. And then the Emperor had defeated the Rouran leader, and for years, there had been no sign of the fearsome

Shadow Warriors. The Empire had gone back to believing it was safe.

But Böri Khan was about to show them how wrong they were to believe the Rourans had been destroyed. His father had taught him all he knew before the Emperor had killed him. And now Böri Khan had revitalized the Rourans. It was time, he thought as his eyes flicked to the open gate of the trading post, for them to begin their revenge.

Turning to his warriors, Böri Khan raised his hand. Twelve horses shifted on their feet as the twelve men, dressed in black, their faces covered except for a slit for their eyes, tightened their legs as they prepared to urge their mounts forward. In the hand of one of the warriors was a pole. A black-and-gold flag flew from it, bearing the head of a wolf waving and undulating in the light breeze. Böri Khan waited a moment more. He wanted to see the fear in the eyes of the guards when they noticed him and his men.

He did not have to wait long. Up on top of the wall, a guard turned the corner. In the same moment, the wind whipped up, snapping the wolf banner. The sound carried across the steppe and the guard spotted Böri Khan and his warriors.

A smile of satisfaction spread over the Rouran leader's face as he saw panic fill the guard's eyes. As the guard began a fruitless attempt to warn the other soldiers and close the marketplace gates, Böri Khan dropped his arm.

In an instant, the Shadow Warriors raced across the desert. Their horses' hooves pounded on the sand, creating a huge cloud of dust behind them. The giant beasts ate up the distance and soon were upon the trading post. Up on the wall, guards began to let loose arrows. But their aim was off, their hands shaky. The arrows flew wide and short and the Shadow Warriors galloped closer.

"Take out the leader!" Böri Khan heard one of the guards shout. Lifting his eyes, he saw another guard take aim. Böri Khan didn't hesitate. He kept charging forward, even as the arrow flew straight toward his chest. Just as it was about to impale him, he lifted his hands, grabbing the arrow by the shaft and stopping it. As the guards' jaws dropped, Böri Khan pulled his own bow from his back and notched the arrow. He let it loose.

To the guards' surprise, the arrow didn't fly toward a person but rather arced through the sky, sailing over the wall before embedding with a loud

THWIP in a pole in the middle of the marketplace. The merchants and traders, who had been unaware of the approaching danger, looked over at the arrow in alarm.

Standing nearby, a trader wearing a red fez shifted his eyes to the arrow. A calculating glint flashed in his eye as he lifted his hand and slowly pulled a long needle from behind his ear. Then, with a cry, he kicked over a spice stand. As colored powder filled the air, the man in the red fez began to transform. His hair grew longer and began to flow over his shoulders, and his features began to morph. His cheeks thinned and his skin grew smooth. Under his cloak, his waist narrowed. A few merchants shouted as the transformation came to an end.

Where the man in the red fez had just been now stood a beautiful—and dangerous-looking—woman. But this was no ordinary woman. This was Xianniang.

"Witch!" shouted one of the guards whose attention had been pulled from Böri Khan to the center of the marketplace. "She's a witch!"

At his shout, the marketplace erupted in panic.

Traders and merchants pushed and shoved at each other, trying to get out of the way of the witch. The air filled with dirt from the stampeding feet. Standing in the middle of the commotion, unmoving and unconcerned, Xianniang watched the chaos unfold.

Slowly she bent her knees and raised one arm. With her other arm, she reached into her belt and then, fast as lightning, pulled out four daggers. With a hawklike shriek the witch let the daggers fly. One by one, they soared across the marketplace, hitting four guards and knocking them to the ground.

Up on the wall, the other guards barely had time to register their fallen comrades. They were too busy dealing with Böri Khan. Beneath him, his stallion's strides went unchecked despite the flying arrows and chaos around him. With breakneck speed, the horse approached the wall. On its back, Böri Khan grabbed a handful of mane. Then, in one smooth move, he vaulted himself from a seated position so that he was standing atop his horse's back. He unsheathed his sword and waited, his legs steady despite the galloping steed beneath him. Just when it looked as though he were going to race headlong into the wall, Böri Khan leapt.

Flying through the air, his legs pumped as though he were running. Determination—and anger—filled his face, and with a mighty roar, he landed atop the wall. The guards were no match for Khan's slashing sword. The metal became a blur as he whipped it back and forth with practiced ease.

Taking the cue from their leader, the other Shadow Warriors clambered up onto the wall and attacked. The clang of sword against sword rang out as the warriors and the guards battled.

Spotting Xianniang in the marketplace, Böri Khan dispatched two more charging guards and then jumped down to the marketplace wall. Unaware of his presence, the witch continued her own fight. Surrounded by five soldiers, all bigger and stronger than her, Xianniang was unbothered. Her face was a mask of calm, her hands steady. She seemed to be waiting for them to make the first move, even though she was heavily outnumbered.

Seeing their own advantage, the guards signaled to one another. Then they attacked. They lashed out with long spears, but the ends of their weapons met nothing but air. In the blink of an eye, Xianniang grabbed hold of the nearest spear and flipped it back on the men. Her body became a blur of black silk as she whipped and turned and spun. When she stopped moving, four of the soldiers lay on the ground. The fifth was on his knees, shaking. Younger than the others, he looked up at Xianniang's focused gaze, his own eyes filled with terror.

Böri Khan stepped forward. Sensing his presence, the witch looked over. Their eyes met. Then, ever so slowly, Xianniang lowered her spear. Böri Khan nodded. Their plan, the plan he had kept even from his own men, had worked. He was pleased. The others had doubted the witch would stick by him, but he had known better. Xianniang was powerful, but she was power hungry, too. A life of solitude, kept on the outside of a society fearful of her kind, too often forced to transform into her hawk form to avoid judgment, or worse, punishment, had made her angry and bent on revenge. And now they were one step closer. The garrison was theirs.

Together, Xianniang and Böri Khan walked back

toward the gate. Behind them, the battle sounds dimmed as the Shadow Warriors took down the remaining guards.

"Another garrison falls, Böri Khan," Xianniang said, her voice raspy but her breath even.

The warrior nodded. The Emperor would not be able to ignore him any longer. The Rourans were back—and soon the Empire would be theirs.

FOUR

Inside the walls of the Imperial City, daily life was going on much as it always did—peacefully. The huge city, nearly thirty square miles of streets laid out in perfect grids, was a bastion of civilization. In stark contrast to the dusty, loud, and somewhat chaotic nature of the trading garrison, the city looked every bit the cosmopolitan center it had come to be. The citizens who made the Imperial City their home took pride in the markets that bustled with international traders. Temples could be found in nearly every section of the city, their presence a calming reminder of the ancestors who watched over the people and put their trust and power in the Emperor. Boulevards were lined with elegant estates, and city planners had made sure that green parks were prominent, adding to the sense of serenity. Boat-filled canals and harbors broke up the otherwise lush landscape.

In the northwest corner, looking over the city from atop a hill, stood the Imperial Palace. Home to the Emperor, it was the grandest building in the entire city. White and gold, it looked as if it had been freshly painted that very morning. Brightly colored birds flew over its gate, landing to nest in the branches of the many trees that surrounded the building. From a distance or up close, the palace was made to inspire peace and confidence.

And it did both. Usually.

Inside the throne room, the Chancellor looked up at the Emperor, who sat on his throne, his face unreadable. He felt, as he always did in the massive space, dwarfed and a bit insignificant. But he knew that he wasn't. After decades of working at the Emperor's side, he was the man's most trusted advisor. Which meant he knew that the news he was about to deliver was going to upset the Emperor greatly.

Taking a deep breath and bowing his head, the Chancellor stepped forward. "Your Majesty," he began, hoping his voice didn't sound as shaky as he felt, "six of our northern garrisons along the Silk Road have fallen in a coordinated attack." The dozens of official scribes who surrounded the leader kept their heads down, but the Chancellor saw them shift nervously on their feet. The Emperor himself remained silent, his body in shadow. The Chancellor went on. "All trade in the northern region has been disrupted."

"And my citizens?" the Emperor asked, his voice low.

"Slaughtered," the Chancellor replied. "This soldier is the only survivor." He nodded to a young man who was kneeling nearby. Even from a distance, the Chancellor could see the guard's face was drawn and pale. What he had seen at the garrison had been, in his own words, nightmarish.

He had spoken of a winged witch and fierce warriors. Even just thinking about it made the hairs on the Chancellor's arms rise. "I fear more attacks will follow."

Standing up, the Emperor stepped out of the shadows. While not a towering figure, the Emperor exuded power nonetheless. His eyes were bright and wise, and only a few age lines could be seen despite the responsibility he carried. Even though the news had clearly pained him, the Emperor remained calm. It was that trait, among many others, that made him such a beloved leader.

"Who is responsible?" he asked.

The answer stuck in the Chancellor's throat as he felt the Emperor's gaze on him. It was nearly impossible for him to hide his emotions from the other man. "Rourans, Your Majesty," he said at last, the words barely a whisper.

But they were loud enough. A wave of shock swept across the room as the scribes began to whisper among themselves.

The Emperor ignored them. "Who leads them?" he asked.

"He calls himself Böri Khan," the Chancellor answered.

"I killed Böri Khan," the Emperor said, his voice beginning to sound strained.

"His son, Your Majesty."

The Emperor shook his head. The Chancellor knew what he was thinking. There was no way that was possible. How could a child of the man he had personally killed manage to resurrect an entire army? He had spent years working to make sure the Rouran forces would never rise again. He had nearly lost his life dozens of times and yet now they were back? He shook his head again, struggling to control his breathing, which was starting to grow ragged. "They were *destroyed*," he said, his voice loud, the sound echoing off the walls of the throne room. "I ask again: How is it possible?"

Before the Chancellor could respond, a small voice rose up. Looking over in surprise, the Chancellor saw that the lone survivor of the garrison attack had gotten to his feet. "You may speak," the Chancellor said to the guard.

"Böri Khan fights alongside a witch," the guard said.

This time, no one tried to hold back their gasps. The sound filled the room. This was terrible news.

"There is *no* place for witches in this kingdom!"

the Chancellor shouted. "Sorcery was outlawed over a hundred years ago." His outburst surprised even himself. The Chancellor had honed his skills at keeping his emotions hidden. But witches? Witches made his blood boil.

"And yet," the guard said, with the slightest shrug of his shoulders, "it is her skill that leads the Rouran army to victory."

"How do you know this?" the Emperor asked, stepping forward and causing his guards and scribes to scurry after him. Moving farther into the throne room, the Emperor seemed to grow larger. And despite his own chancellor's obvious anger, the Emperor remained calm.

"I only know what I saw with my own eyes," the guard answered. "The witch is powerful."

For a long moment, the Emperor stood still, his face betraying nothing. But watching him, the Chancellor knew the man's mind was busy. There was no denying it. The Rourans were back, with a new leader. A leader who, like his father, wanted nothing more than to destroy the Empire. And this time, the Rouran had the help of a powerful witch. The Chancellor didn't need a priestess to tell him what these signs meant. They meant chaos. They meant war. They meant an end to the peace the Emperor had worked so hard to achieve.

As if hearing his chancellor—and friend's—thoughts, the Emperor lifted his eyes. He looked toward the distant window and the Empire on display beyond. "We are not afraid of dark magic," he said. "We will destroy this Rouran army—and their witch." As he went on, the Emperor's voice grew louder, stronger. "Here is my decree: We will raise a mighty army. Every family will supply one man. We will protect our beloved people and *crush* these murderers."

His decree complete, the scribes around him frantically wrote down his words. It would be their job to deliver his decree to the people of the Empire. And as it was decided, no family would be allowed to object. The Emperor would have his army.

Watching the court bustle into frantic motion at the Emperor's decree, the young guard who had narrowly escaped the Rourans moved toward the exit. With a nod to the Chancellor, who was in the middle of speaking to several scribes at once and barely acknowledged him, the guard made his way through the long throne room and out into the hall.

As he moved along, his shoulders straightened. His head, which he had kept bowed the entire time he had been in the presence of the Emperor, rose. Stride by stride, his gait began to change. By the time he reached the palace exit and had made his way onto the busy streets, he was walking swiftly, with no sign of the injuries inflicted by the Rourans.

People of all nationalities passed by him, some nodding at his uniform, a few young women even smiling slightly. But he paid them no heed. As he turned down an alley, his pace eased. Reaching up a hand, he removed a pin that had been hidden behind his ear and let it drop to the ground. As he walked, more pins fell around his feet. Soon the ground was littered with the pins—along with the guard's unconscious body. Standing above it, no longer in need of the man's form, stood the witch. Xianniang stretched, happy to be back in her own shape. Then, with a careless glance at the guard who had unwittingly just helped her cause, she ran.

Faster and faster her footsteps came and then, with a cry, she leapt. As her body lifted into the air, it once again transformed. Only this time, instead of the guard, she became a giant, graceful hawk. As she soared up and over the city, Xianniang let out a triumphant caw. Böri Khan would be pleased. She had seen the flash of fear in the Emperor's eyes when she had mentioned the warrior's name. Raising an army of civilians was just what Böri Khan had hoped for. Leave the villages empty of their strongest men. It would make taking them over all the easier.

FIVE

Mulan was miserable. Sitting on an uncomfortable stool, she tried not to move as her mother gathered her long black hair and tugged and pulled the strands into submission. Mulan winced as a few more tangled strands gave up their fight and were yanked painfully from her head.

She had anticipated the process of meeting the Matchmaker would be emotionally exhausting, but she had failed to consider the physical toll it would take on her body. Of course she couldn't just arrive to be interviewed by the esteemed Matchmaker in just any old thing. No, no, no, her mother had said, disgusted by the mere idea of it when Mulan had mentioned it. "One must present herself to the Matchmaker as she would to her suitor—perfectly. We *all* must be perfect." And then, as if Mulan didn't know it already, her mother added, "Our family's fortune rests on you, Mulan."

Which was why Mulan now found herself being made up to look like a porcelain doll. Satisfied by the buns piled high on Mulan's head, Li turned her attention to her daughter's face. Bowls had been laid out on a nearby table, each filled with different powders and liquids. Dipping a thicker brush into the nearest bowl, Li stirred the white paste. Then she brushed it in smooth, even strokes over Mulan's face. When the girl's face was completely covered, Li moved on to the next bowl. Yellow powder was blown gently onto Mulan's forehead, returning some color to her face and making Mulan wonder why they bothered painting it bright white in the first place. But before she could even open her mouth to ask, Li put down the yellow powder and picked up the blue ink. That was added above Mulan's eyes, becoming long, thin "eyebrows" that tilted up at the ends so the girl seemed to be smiling even though her mouth was straight. Rouge was added to Mulan's cheeks, red was painted on her lips, and finally Li pasted a golden ornament between her daughter's eyes.

Her face addressed, Mulan was pulled off the chair and forced to stand while her mother dressed her. Mulan remained silent, though she felt more and more like screaming. Her mother hadn't dressed her since she was a girl. She had never been forced to wear face paint and her head already hurt from the dozens of pins shoved into her hair to keep the buns in place. She felt like a doll her sister would have played with when she was a girl.

Mulan's gaze shifted to the window on the far wall. Through it she could see Black Wind grazing. She wanted to burst free from her mother's grasp and run outside, leap on her horse's back, and race off. But she knew she could not. She had made her promise and she would not let her family down—again.

"Look."

Her mother's voice startled Mulan and she brought her gaze back into the room. She gasped as she saw her reflection in the mirror her mother held out. The face that stared back was that of a stranger. Her body, wrapped in a lilac-colored dress, looked strange: curves were visible that were usually hidden under loose clothing. Gingerly, Mulan lifted her head and touched the lotus flower comb her mother had placed in her hair. The comb was one of her mother's most cherished possessions. Without saying anything, Li was reminding Mulan just how important today was.

Taking a deep breath, Mulan headed out of the house and into the courtyard. Her father stood waiting, also in his own formal attire. Seeing his eldest daughter, he smiled, but not before Mulan caught a flash of sadness in his eyes. At least she wasn't the only one who felt she was hiding her real self under a pile of makeup.

As soon as Li and Xiu joined them, both also dressed up though neither looked quite as exquisite as Mulan, the family began to walk through the village. Passing by people she had known her entire life, Mulan felt their eyes on her and heard the surprised whispers as they walked by. Although

Mulan *felt* unrecognizable, the villagers seemed to recognize her nonetheless.

Sensing his daughter's discomfort, Zhou smiled warmly. He stopped and looked at his family. "I am truly blessed to be in the presence of such enchanting women," he said. "I have no doubt that today will be a momentous day for the Hua fam—"

"Never mind that," his wife said, cutting him off. "We must be on time." To emphasize her words, she resumed walking, her pace quicker.

Behind her, Mulan struggled to keep up. Her dress was meant to look pretty; it was not meant to be jogged in. And her feet were bound in tight and uncomfortable shoes. She nearly toppled over and would have had her sister not reached out and steadied her. Then, as if on cue, Mulan's stomach growled loudly.

"I'm starving," she said, stating the obvious.

Li rolled her eyes impatiently. "I have already told you—you cannot eat. It will ruin your makeup."

"The fiercest winter storm could not destroy this makeup," Mulan retorted under her breath. Turning to her sister, Mulan saw that her mother's anxiety had rubbed off on Xiu. The younger girl was wringing her hands nervously. "Xiu," Mulan said, trying to lighten the mood. She pointed to her face. "What am I feeling?"

Xiu looked at her, her eyes searching Mulan's face for any trace of emotion. "I have no idea," she said.

"Exactly," Mulan answered. "This is my sad face." The expression on her painted face did not change. "This is my curious face." Still no change. "Now I am confused." Once more, her face remained the same.

At last, a smile began to break over Xiu's face. Mulan smiled back—even though her sister couldn't tell. She hated to think that the cause of all this anxiety was her, but she knew that was the case. If it had been Xiu on her way to meet the Matchmaker, Li would have been practically skipping. Xiu gave her mother and family no reason to worry. Mulan gave her mother and family *only* reason to worry.

Luckily, Mulan didn't have time to dwell on her insufficiencies. They had arrived at the Matchmaker's house. Leaving Zhou to wait outside, the women approached the front door.

As befit a woman of status, the Matchmaker's house stood alone. The sides were newly painted, and fresh flowers and herbs blossomed on either side of the door. The Matchmaker was one of the most important people in their small village. It was her connections that kept the young ladies and men matching and, in turn, the village thriving. Families spent a great deal of time trying to earn her approval, as favor from the Matchmaker inevitably meant a favorable match.

Despite the constant doting and the privilege that came with her position, the Matchmaker was a mean and nasty woman. When she left her house, which wasn't often, she always wore a frown full of judgment. Mulan had, on more than one occasion, turned and walked the other way when she saw the Matchmaker in order to avoid a glare from the large woman. And Xiu, when she was younger and before she knew better, had once remarked how it wasn't fair that such a beautiful house had such an ugly owner.

But it didn't matter if the woman was mean and her frown ugly. She held Mulan's future in her hands.

The Matchmaker, after introducing Mulan to Fong Lin, the mother of her prospective match, nodded for everyone to sit. Quickly, Mulan and her family sat. For one long moment, silence filled the small room and Mulan wished that she had a rag or something to wipe her sweaty palms on. She knew what she was supposed to do. Pour tea. Prove that she was worthy of Fong Lin's son. It seemed easy in theory . . . *if* Mulan could stop her hands from shaking.

Be calm, she reminded herself. *Remember what Xiu told you—picture doing something you like. Just get the tea in the cups. That's all you have to do.*

Slowly, Mulan reached out a hand and lifted the delicate porcelain teapot. As she began to pour the steaming liquid into the equally delicate cups—without spilling—she could almost hear her mother's shoulders sag in relief.

Obviously pleased as well, the Matchmaker began to speak. "Quiet. Demure. Graceful," she listed. "These are the qualities we see in a good wife." She paused and looked directly at Fong Lin. The woman, whose quiet judgment Mulan had felt like daggers, did not move a muscle or blink. Her eyes bored into Mulan, watching every move with fierce attention to detail. "These are the qualities we see in Mulan."

Be calm, Mulan repeated to herself. *Calm. Be calm*

even though this woman seems terrible and therefore probably has a terrible son who is going to give you the same terrible look every time you do something you shouldn't, which will be always. Because you are not, let's face it, quiet, demure, or graceful. Stopping herself, Mulan put the teapot down and moved on to the sugar. She felt everyone's eyes on her as she moved around the table, from cup to cup.

"They say," the Matchmaker went on, not bothered or nonplussed by Fong Lin's blank look, "that when a wife serves her husband, she must be silent. She must be invisible." She stopped. Her eyes focused on Mulan, looking for the slightest hint of a tremor, the smallest exhale of breath. Mulan was silent.

As she put a final cube of sugar into the last cup, Mulan returned to her seat. She had done it. Not a drop spilled. Not a mess made. Still, she wouldn't allow herself the chance to sigh in relief. Not yet.

"The Fong family honors the Hua family with this exquisite tea set," the Matchmaker went on, a glimmer of approval in her eyes. "A gift from the Imperial Family."

Mulan, Li, and Xiu bowed their heads

in gratitude. While it was tradition for the Matchmaker to not reveal details to either family about the other family, there was always a way to glean a little bit. In this case, as Mulan stared at the beautiful teapot on the table in front of her, she knew that Fong Lin's family was well-off, at least more so than hers. The Huas' teapot was faded and their cups mismatched. This new one would stand out on their threadbare shelves. The pressure to be perfect felt even greater. Mulan's family would benefit from her marriage to a successful man. She *had* to pull this off.

Mulan was just starting to believe she could get through the meeting when she looked over at Xiu. Her younger sister's eyes were wide with fear. Following her gaze, Mulan saw a large spider slowly unspooling itself from the ceiling toward the table. Inch by inch it made its way down . . . right toward Xiu. It dropped onto the table, its long, hairy legs undulating beneath it.

Underneath her mask of white makeup, Mulan felt the color drain from her face. If the spider took even one step toward Xiu, the girl was certain to scream and the Matchmaker would be furious. Smoothly, and thankful for the mask her makeup provided, Mulan reached out and placed the teapot over the spider. Then she returned her hands to her lap. But not before shooting her sister a look.

The look, unfortunately, was not lost on the Matchmaker. Her own eyes narrowed. "Is something wrong?" she asked.

"No, Madam Matchmaker," Mulan said in her most demure voice. "Thank you."

The Matchmaker's lips tightened in unspoken aggravation. Mulan met her gaze, her own expression revealing nothing. Finally, the Matchmaker nodded toward the teapot. "It is ideal," she said, her tone dripping with condescension, "for the teapot to remain in the center of the table."

"Yes," Mulan agreed. "I understand. But I think the teapot should remain where it is."

Instantly, the room grew icy. A sheen of sweat appeared on Li's brow and Xiu's breath stopped, her face growing as white as Mulan's painted one. Fong Lin looked back and forth between the Matchmaker and Mulan, perplexed.

"Move the teapot, girl." Each word shot out of the Matchmaker's mouth like an arrow.

Mulan looked back and forth between the

teapot and her sister, unsure what to do. If she moved the pot, the spider would move, too. But if she *didn't* move the pot, then things wouldn't end well anyway. She thought of her father, standing outside, waiting for her to keep her promise. She sighed. She had to do what the Matchmaker said.

Slowly, she lifted the teapot.

The spider, released from its makeshift prison, leapt—right into the lap of Fong Lin.

Letting out an ear-piercing shriek, Fong Lin jumped to her feet, brushing wildly at her lap and sending the spider flying. For one beat, the room grew still again as the women all looked to see where the spider had landed. . . .

And then the Matchmaker let out a scream of her own as she looked down and saw the creature crawling across her chest. Terrified, she stumbled backward, her arms pinwheeling wildly. The momentum sent her tumbling into a chair. Her feet, kicking furiously, contacted the table, flipping it up. The teapot and teacups were sent flying, end over end, shooting hot water in every direction as they spun.

Watching as the room devolved into absolute chaos around her, Mulan stayed eerily still. Her eyes were the only thing that moved as they tracked the arc of the teapot and cups. Then, in a blur of motion, she reached up and pulled out the four long pins that held up her hair. Extending one of the pins, she caught a teacup. Then another. *Clink. Clink. Clink.* One by one, she snagged the other teapots out of midair, balancing them on the pins.

But the teapot was still falling. Looking over, Mulan saw it was mere inches from hitting the floor. Mulan didn't stop to think. She just acted. Quick as lightning, she stuck out her foot. She grimaced as she heard her dress rip, but the handle of the pot snagged on her toe. It hung, dangling precariously as the teacups continued to swing on the pins.

For one long moment, the room was silent. Mulan felt the eyes of the four other women on her, their surprise mirroring her own. She had done it. She had averted disaster. The spider was gone and the tea set was in one piece.

And then, her long thick hair, freed from the pins that had kept it contained, began to escape its buns. Like water pouring from the top of a falls, it dropped down, the long strands covering Mulan's face.

With her vision blocked, Mulan had nothing to focus on. Almost instantly, she lost her balance. The leg on the ground began to shake while the one in the air began to sway. Then her arms followed suit, moving up and down and side to side until, with a shout, Mulan fell.

Crash! Crash! Crash!

Piece by piece the tea set smashed to the ground, breaking into a thousand fragments.

Lying on the floor, Mulan heard Fong Lin's shriek of rage and felt the look of disappointment coming from her own mother. Xiu was weeping quietly as she leaned down and tried to pick up the larger pieces of porcelain. But even the gentlest of touches broke the pieces still smaller, causing Fong Lin to scream again. A moment later, Mulan heard the front door open and then slam as the mother of her suitor—or rather, ex-suitor—stormed outside.

Mulan got to her feet, her head still bowed. She followed Fong Lin's departure, her mother and sister joining her. None of them said a word. They walked in silence out the door, down the front stairs, and into the courtyard where Zhou waited.

But the Matchmaker was not nearly as quiet.

Storming out from behind them, she lifted her arm and pointed an accusatory finger right at Mulan. "Dishonor to the Hua family!" she screamed, her voice bouncing off the walls of the nearby houses and catching the attention of the entire village. "They have failed to raise a good daughter!"

Each word was like a slap across Mulan's face. The Matchmaker was right. She had failed her family. She would never bring them honor. How could she, now that the Matchmaker would never let her step foot in her house again?

Not daring to meet her father's gaze, unable to face the disappointment she knew she would see, Mulan began to trudge across the courtyard and back to her own home. It was going to be the longest walk of her life with nothing but her sad thoughts and angry looks from her mother for company. In that second, Mulan wished for anything, anything at all, to take the attention from her.

As if on cue, the sound of drumbeats began to echo through the village.

Mulan and her family, along with the entire village, stopped in their tracks. All eyes turned toward the single-lane road that led into their small village. Normally it was empty, the dirt undisturbed. But now they could see billowing sand kicked into the air by what appeared to be a small parade of riders.

A few of the younger children raced ahead to see what was happening and turned around. "Soldiers!" they shouted as they ran back.

Mulan's heart pounded in her chest as around her, the villagers began to murmur among themselves. It had been years since soldiers had appeared in their village. The last time had been when her own father had been taken off to fight for the Emperor. What could they be doing there now?

Just then, the drumming stopped and the dust settled. There, standing in front of them, were a magistrate and six soldiers. The men looked at the villagers from atop their horses, their faces hidden by masks. With a signal from the magistrate, several of them jumped down and began to post pieces of paper to various houses.

"Citizens! Citizens!" the magistrate shouted, as if he hadn't already gotten everyone's attention. "We are under attack from northern invaders. Our land is at war! By edict of His Imperial Majesty the Son of Heaven, every family must contribute one man to fight! One man from every house!" He pulled out a scroll and unrolled it. From where she stood, Mulan could see that the writing on the scroll was a long list of names. "Wang family! Chin family!"

As the magistrate continued to read off the list of the families who lived in the tulou, Mulan realized her father had disappeared into the crowd. She rose on her tiptoes, trying to see where he had gone, but the village had devolved into chaos. Men were pushing their way through the crowd to get the paperwork that would conscript them into the army. Behind them, women old and young started to weep, some out of joy that one man from their family would be a hero, and others because they knew the consequences of war—both physically and mentally.

"Du family! Hua family!"

Mulan's breath caught in her throat when she heard her family's name called. She looked for her father, spotting him making his way through the crowd. He walked with his head held high and without the use of his cane. Mulan knew what he was about to do.

Approaching the magistrate and two of the

soldiers who had remained on horseback, Zhou bowed. "I am Hua Zhou," he said as he rose back up. "I served the Imperial Army in the last battle against the northern invaders."

The magistrate looked down at Zhou. "Have you no son old enough to fight?" he asked.

"I am blessed with two daughters," Mulan's father answered. "I will fight."

The magistrate considered the man before him. Mulan saw him eyeing her father's graying hair and the lines at his eyes. She knew that to him, her father appeared a proud, but old, man. Finally, the magistrate nodded to the soldier nearest him. The young man reached into his bag and pulled out a set of papers that would mark Zhou for service. He held it out.

In what felt like slow motion, Mulan watched as her father reached out his own hand. His fingers brushed the parchment and were about to close around the paper when his leg gave out. He gave a muffled shout as he fell to the ground. Lying at the feet of the magistrate's horse, Zhou's eyes closed in horror. His waistcoat had fallen open, revealing the binding on his leg that now, due to the fall, was unraveling.

Looking at her father, Mulan's heart broke. The man was utterly humiliated. Even the soldiers seemed embarrassed for him, stepping back and then averting their eyes. Spotting her father's cane lying on the ground where he must have left it, Mulan moved to take it. But her mother put a hand on her shoulder, stopping her.

"You must not," she whispered. "That will only humiliate him further."

As the magistrate resumed reading the names of the tulou families, a younger soldier dismounted and offered his hand to Zhou. Zhou refused. Grasping his scroll tightly in his hand, he painfully pushed himself to his feet. Then he limped away, his head high.

Mulan watched him go. Her father was a good man, but he was a proud man. And that pride was going to get him killed if he went to war.

SIX

A sense of impending doom hung over the Hua household. They had managed to ignore the events of the afternoon for the rest of the day, but now, as they gathered around the dinner table, the tension was thick.

Mulan played with her food. She had no appetite. How could she when there was a rock in the middle of her stomach from the thought of her father fighting the northern invaders? Beside her, Xiu took a half-hearted bite and then put down her food. She wasn't hungry, either.

Across the way, Mulan's mother hadn't even bothered to take a plate. She sat with her eyes locked on Zhou. Unaware, or choosing to ignore the looks from his wife and daughters, Zhou ate with gusto.

"You're a war hero," Li said, her words soft as she broke the silence. "You've already made many great sacrifices—"

Zhou didn't let her finish. He knew what she was going to say. "Are you suggesting our family not comply with the Imperial edict?"

The words were out of Mulan's mouth before she could stop them. "But how can you fight when you can barely—"

Zhou's fist slammed onto the table, stopping Mulan midsentence. Fury filled his face. His wife and daughters looked at him aghast. He had always been a man who prided himself on restraint and keeping his calm. This outburst was unlike him— and it was frightening.

"I am the *father*!" he said, his voice booming through the small room. "It is my place to bring honor to our family on the battlefield. You are the *daughter.*" He paused, his eyes boring into Mulan. *"Learn your place!"* Pushing himself to his feet, Zhou limped from the room.

At the table, Mulan sat still, her head hung low. Her father's words stung. Not just because of their tone, but because of the meaning behind them. Her father had always been her biggest supporter. He had always encouraged her to be who she was; even when she was trying to hide her impetuous nature, she had still felt his love and encouragement. She had always believed her father knew that she wanted more, could be more.

But she had been wrong.

And worse still, his stubborn pride was going to put him in mortal danger.

As if reading her thoughts, Li stood up and walked over to her daughter's side of the table. She grabbed Mulan's hand and then Xiu's. "We must be strong," she said. She paused. And then her eyes welled and her hands shook. Even she could not follow her own orders. "This time he will not return," she said, letting the tears fall. Her shoulders slumped and she sank to the ground, overcome by emotion. "How will we survive with-out him?"

Mulan looked at her distraught mother and then at her sister. Both were now openly weeping. Her mother was right. If her father went to fight, he would die. If her father died, he would leave them with nothing. And as Mulan had just destroyed her one chance at a match, there was no hope for a future husband to help their family if Zhou were gone.

The truth was clear. If Zhou went to war, *none* of them would survive it.

The house had grown quiet. The sounds of her mother's sobs had faded, and her sister, tears drying on her cheeks, had fallen into a restless sleep as Mulan tiptoed across the living area toward the large cabinet that stood in the corner. The ornate piece was one of the only items of worth in their home. When she was a girl, Mulan had been forbidden to go near it, and even as a young woman she'd kept her distance.

Until tonight.

Mulan took a deep breath. The idea that had

come to her as she lay in bed had started as just a flicker of a thought, as she heard her father's words echo around her head. *Learn your place,* he had said. Her place, she knew, was clear—to her father, at least. Her place was in the home, taking care of a husband she most likely would never have. But what if her place were different? What if she had been born a boy? It would have been *her* place to go fight the invaders. And that was when the idea blossomed. Why couldn't she fight? Who was stopping her? All she needed was a suit of armor, a weapon, and a horse. Well, she had the horse, so that left the weapon and armor.

Which was how she had ended up here, now, standing in front of the family's cabinet.

Slowly she opened the cabinet doors. They squeaked slightly and Mulan froze. When no candle was lit and no noise came from the family's rooms, Mulan let out her breath. Then she opened the doors the rest of the way.

Inside was her father's suit of armor and sword. The very same suit and sword he had worn into battle years ago. They looked brand-new. Her father lovingly cleaned both at least once a week. Mulan's eyes lingered on the sword. In the light from the lantern at her feet, the metal seemed to burn with an internal fire.

Mulan pulled the sword free from its display. Her hands dropped under the surprising weight and she shifted to keep her balance. She stayed still for a moment, getting used to the heft and feel of the metal in her hands. Her father had, on the rare occasion his leg wasn't bothering him, taken the sword out and practiced in the yard. He had made the movements seem so fluid that Mulan had always assumed the sword was light as a feather. But in her hand, it was heavy and awkward. As she tried to lift it straight in front of her, her eyes flickered over three words etched into the blade itself. Squinting, she read: LOYAL. BRAVE. TRUE.

As the moon moved from behind a cloud, the room filled with white light. In that moment, Mulan caught her own reflection in the steel of the blade. As she turned the sword this way and that, her features changed. Her cheeks grew sharper, her eyes wider, her lips thinner. She looked like a different version of herself.

What was a hint of an idea began to grow. Why couldn't she be herself—and someone else—at the same time? Why couldn't she take her father's place? She had everything she needed right there in front of her. She could be a soldier. She lowered her arms and stretched the sword out in front of her, her eyes as steely and strong as the weapon itself.

Mulan was no longer going to let others decide her future. She had tried to keep her promise to bring honor to her family by parading in front of the Matchmaker. She had, for years, practiced her weaving. She had learned to be silent and rein in her wildest impulses. She had practiced pouring tea and made countless dinners. Yet no matter how hard she tried, she had always seemed to fall short. So now she would bring honor to her family in another way.

She would become a warrior.

Holding the hilt of the sword in one hand and awkwardly carrying the armor under her other arm, Mulan made her way back across the living room. Passing by her parents' slightly open bedroom door, she could see her father's face, stubborn even in sleep. Beside him, Li slept fitfully, worry creasing her forehead. Mulan wished she could wake them and tell them goodbye. She wished she could tell them how much she loved them and how much she wanted to make them proud and keep them safe. But instead, she made her way upstairs.

Throwing a few things in a small satchel, she hesitated in the doorway. In her sleep, Xiu let out a small whimper. A fierce wave of love rushed through Mulan. She knew that the moment she stepped out of their house, she would risk never coming back. Even if she was to survive the army, which she very well might not, her reputation was unlikely to survive what she was about to attempt: pretending to be a man to fight a war she had no place in. She knew the odds were against her, but she also knew she couldn't let her father go in her stead.

He had been right. She had to learn her place. But that place wasn't here.

The sound of thunder woke Zhou. Stirring under the covers, he turned his head and looked through the window at the ominous gray sky. Something fluttered in his belly, and his leg, which ached on a good day, pounded with the impending weather. Something was wrong. He knew it.

Pushing off the sheets, he lowered his feet to the floor and tiptoed out of the room. A boom of thunder echoed through the house, and Zhou froze as Li stirred in bed. When she settled, he began to tiptoe once more.

As he entered the living room, the feeling in his stomach worsened. Across the way, he saw the cabinet with its doors slightly ajar. His fear growing, he walked over to the cabinet and swung open the doors.

It was empty.

Zhou gasped. "My sword and armor!" he said. "They're gone." The words were loud, the emotion behind them thick. Hearing footsteps behind him, he didn't even turn as Li entered the room and raced over.

"Who would do such a thing?" Li asked as she, too, took in the empty cabinet and then her husband's pale face and shaking hands.

Awoken by the commotion, Xiu appeared in the doorway. She rubbed her eyes, still half asleep. She barely registered the empty cabinet. Instead, she noticed something—or rather *someone*—else that was missing. "Where is Mulan?" she asked.

Mulan. Zhou took another ragged breath. What did Xiu mean? Mulan was in her bed, where she was supposed to be. But a look at Xiu told him he was wrong. A thought, one that he desperately didn't want to be thinking, began to take shape. His own words yelled in frustration and anger echoed back to him. *Learn your place*, he had said. He had seen the hurt on Mulan's face, but in the moment, he had been too absorbed in his own pain to care. But now . . .

Turning from the cabinet, he searched the small living area. Watching him, Li raised an eyebrow. "My conscription scroll," he said, answering her unasked question. He had to find it. If he couldn't, it could only mean one thing. He brushed aside the plates and empty bowls, looking for the paper that he had left there hours earlier.

But it was gone. In its place was Mulan's lotus comb.

Zhou raised his eyes, his gaze meeting Li's. The terror he felt was mirrored on his wife's face. They understood what the missing armor and conscription scroll meant.

"You must stop her," Li said, holding a trembling hand to her heart. "The northern invaders will kill her!"

Zhou bowed his head. Mulan had never wielded a sword in anything but play, and even then it had been a stick, not a real weapon. She would fall in the first fight. But if he went after her and exposed her lie, her fate would be the same. Her own people, the other soldiers and the leaders of the army, would never let her live if they found out she had betrayed them. He could not stop her.

Leaving his wife and daughter weeping, Zhou exited the house and made his way to the phoenix shrine. He didn't hear the thunder or see the lightning. His head was too full of grief. He had done this. He had pushed Mulan away and sent her to her death.

Entering the small shrine, he kneeled in front of two large tablets. The spirit tablets were said to hold the wisdom and spirits of all the ancestors who had come before. They were supposed to hear and answer prayers. He had to hope that they heard his now. "Ancestors," he whispered. "I . . . I ask for your help. My daughter has made a terrible mistake. Please protect her."

His prayer done, he let the tears fall. Behind him the storm arrived. And somewhere out there—alone—was his daughter. *Mulan,* he thought, *I'm so sorry. Please come back.*

With his head lowered, Zhou did not see a small, ugly, and misshapen bird emerge from behind the phoenix statue. One wing hung low and its head was bent at an odd angle. The bird eyed Zhou for a moment and then hopped down from the statue and made its way out of the shrine. It shivered as the first rain touched its feathers, and then, with a resigned sigh, it scurried—one good wing flapping while the other dragged—out of the tulou.

SEVEN

Böri Khan was pleased. His plans were unfolding brilliantly. The Emperor was shaking in his shoes and gathering together a weak army made of civilian boys and old men. Meanwhile, Böri Khan's success had garnered him the attention of all the other Rouran tribes, who had sent their own leaders, known as Tegins, to meet with him as was the ancient custom. Now the Tegins stood inside his large yurt, while outside their banners—the black bear, snow leopard, serpent, red fire, and wild stallion—whipped and snapped in the wind. It was the first time in years that all five of the greatest tribes had gathered in one place.

And it was all because of Böri Khan.

Looking out over the rough group assembled in his yurt, Böri Khan eyed each of the leaders. They stood amid a breathtaking array of treasures stolen by Böri Khan and his men. Piles of silks and scarves and heaps of jewelry littered the room haphazardly, as though Khan had so much treasure he didn't care if it fell to the floor and got trampled upon. He had made sure to provide platters of food and jugs of drink of which a few of the men now partook. However, despite the apparent celebration, the room felt tense. The tribes had come to support Böri Khan, but that didn't mean they supported one another. Their hatred for each other ran deep and true.

"How can I share with Kilifu Tegin?"

Looking over, Böri Khan saw Tulugui Tegin staring daggers at a smaller man across the yurt. Tulugui was perhaps the meanest—or at least most verbal—of the bunch. As the room filled with murmurs, Khan lifted a hand to silence them. Then he nodded for Tulugui to continue.

"He and his people have been raiding our camps since the time of my grandfather's grandfather," Tulugui finished.

Instantly, Kilifu went on the defensive. "The raids began with *your* people," he said, outraged.

"Kilifu is right!" Bati Tegin, the leader of one of the smaller tribes, shouted, jumping in and cutting Tulugui off before he could respond. "Tulugui also raids my camp. I've seen it with my own eyes!"

The yurt erupted in roars. Brought together, old wounds had quickly reopened. Böri Khan watched, letting the other men shout and spew insults. He once again lifted his hand, and with a single shout, he silenced them. "On and on you go, like a basket of vipers biting each other's tails." As he spoke, he took the time to look at each tribal leader. He wanted them all to hear him. "Fighting, tribe against tribe. Do you not see the bounty before you?"

The sound of rustling wings as Xianniang, in her hawk form, flew into the yurt caused the men to flinch. They ducked as the large bird swooped over their heads and landed on a sizable perch. Settling in, she looked out at the men, her gaze making them all shift nervously on their feet. Böri Khan smiled and nodded toward Xianniang. Then he continued. "We are stronger *together*," he said. "The Rouran people. For decades, scattered like leaves on the wind. Now, rising as one." He pointed at the piles of glittering treasure. "This, my friends, is just a small taste of what is to come. From the garrisons ahead, riches will flow like a mighty river." He stopped, letting his words and the sight of the treasure sink in. He walked over to Xianniang's perch and rubbed his fingers along the hawk's smooth feathers. The whole time, he kept his eyes locked on the Tegins, reading their faces.

Finally, Bati Tegin spoke. He had not once looked at the treasure. His eyes had remained locked on the hawk. "Perhaps. But we are relying on a witch."

The hawk's attention turned from Böri Khan to Bati Tegin. Her sharp eyes blinked, and the man shrank backward. Böri Khan noted the man's fear and smiled. He kept his fingers on the hawk as he said, "Make no mistake: the witch serves *me*. And therefore, all of us! She knows who her master is!"

With a flutter of wings, Xianniang transformed. Her feathers disappeared and she stood in front of them in her true form. Her cold eyes took in the leaders, causing the men to shift nervously on their feet. A look of pleasure crossed her face and she turned to Böri Khan. Raising an eyebrow, she spoke. "Please. Continue, my *Khan*," she said. "I am curious what more you have to say."

Böri Khan did not like her tone, but he kept his face neutral. He would deal with her insubordination later. "Xianniang's one of us," he went on. "When we take the Imperial City she will be justly rewarded. As will all of you."

Then a new voice spoke up. "I do not care about witches," Duba Tegin said. The leader of the serpent clan had been silent until now. The others turned, curious to hear what he would say. "My problem lies elsewhere. It is Böri Khan I don't trust. He needs our help to gain the throne. But are we true partners? Or is he using us to get what he wants?" He pointed at the piles of loot on display around the room. "We get riches. Gold, jewels. But how much gold can a nomad carry? The *real* reward is power. When the time comes, Böri Khan will not share his power."

There were a few murmurs from the other leaders. It was a good question. Packing up and moving their yurts when the season changed, or the herds of animals moved on to new grazing pastures, was their way of life. They did not have permanent homes, so they did not have any permanent place to put such material things. But power? That *was* something they could use.

Sensing the turn in the room, Böri Khan lifted his chest. "Everyone has the right to voice his concerns," he said. "Who else here does not trust me?" He paused, letting his words echo through the yurt. The Tegins did not speak, but he could see the doubt that remained in their eyes. He could not have them questioning him. "Duba Tegin's right. Riches are not power. When the kingdom falls, we will divide the power among us."

At his declaration, the Tegins relaxed and nodded their assent. As the other men dug into the food and drink, Böri Khan turned and walked out of the yurt. He was quiet as he made his way up to the rocky outcropping that looked over his larger yurt and the smaller ones of his men. For a long time, he stood there, listening to the sounds of revelry coming from his tent. As the night wore on, the sounds ebbed and flowed until they grew quiet. One by one, the leaders of the tribes made their way out of the yurt. Getting on their horses, they rode off in different directions, heading back to their own camps to report on the night's events.

Böri Khan's eyes followed Duba Tegin as the older man left the yurt. At the sound of footsteps, he looked over as Xianniang appeared. Her eyes were cold as she met his gaze. "Now I know," she said, hugging her arm to her side. "I serve *you*."

"I said it to put them at ease," Böri Khan replied, brushing off the witch's concern. "They fear what they don't understand."

Xianniang raised an eyebrow. The man was still. If not for his moving eyes, he could have been mistaken for a statue. Not for the first time, Xianniang felt fear. There was something dark and terrible about Böri Khan. But she shrugged the fear off as she did every time. She knew her power.

Böri Khan reached over his shoulder and took an arrow out of its quiver. Notching it in the bow, he raised the weapon. "No other Tegins will ask to share power," he said. Aiming the arrow at the back of Duba Tegin, he pulled back the bow and then let it loose.

Xianniang watched as the arrow flew through the air and lodged itself in Duba Tegin's back. The man slumped in the saddle and a moment later fell to the ground. His horse, free of its rider, took off, galloping into the night. "He was right not to trust you," she said.

Lowering his weapon, Böri Khan turned to Xianniang. He looked pleased. Without another word, he walked down the rocky outcropping toward his yurt.

Xianniang watched him go, a frown on her face. She had heard his message. She would not challenge him—not yet, at least.

Mulan was tired. She was tired and hungry. From her spot astride Black Wind, she shook her head, loosening the tension in her neck. Her long hair, which had been tucked under her father's helmet, cascaded down her back. It had been a long, hard ride so far, and already her body ached. She was not used to the weight of the armor or the feel of a sword, or the limited sight she had from under the helmet. But she knew all were necessary if she was going to convince anyone she was a man on his way to war.

It felt like she had been riding for days. And when she wasn't riding, she was walking to give Black Wind a break. She had seen every type of countryside China had to offer. She had wandered through foggy forests and plodded through swampy rivers. Black Wind had galloped them over long stretches of grass, and she had led him over rocky crags.

Now she found herself riding through a bamboo forest. The tall grass rose into the air, its bark smooth. Sunlight filtered through the green canopy, bathing the ground in dim light. It was peaceful, and for the first time since she had left her home, Mulan felt as though she could relax. She let out a deep breath and felt her back loosen. Beneath her, Black Wind nickered, happy to have Mulan's tense legs release some of their pressure on his sides.

SQUAWK!

The awful sound startled Mulan and she pulled back sharply on Black Wind's reins. Turning in the direction of the noise, Mulan saw a small bird dodging in and out of the bamboo. As it came closer, Mulan's lip pulled back. *Bird* was perhaps too generous a description. This creature looked like a big, half-plucked turkey with wings that hung unevenly. Its feathers were dull and faded and its eyes seemed to have trouble focusing. The creature was, all in all, ugly.

Squeezing her legs against Black Wind's sides once again, Mulan urged him forward. The bird, or whatever it was, looked like it was sick. She didn't want to let it get near them.

By the time Mulan pulled Black Wind to a stop for the day, she had almost forgotten about the bird. Making a small fire at the base of an enormous sleeping Buddha statue, she heated up one of the last bits of rice she had and ate the morsels. In no time her meal was over, and with hunger still gnawing at her belly, she crawled into the large open palm of the Buddha and lay down, shivering beneath her thin blanket. Above, she saw the stars twinkling in the sky. Mulan sighed. She had spent so many nights looking at the same stars from her own bed, wishing for an adventure, for a chance to get out of her village.

But now that she was gone, she wished more

than anything to go back home. Pulling the blanket up farther, she whispered good night to Black Wind and closed her eyes. Exhaustion took over and she quickly fell asleep . . . so she was not awake to see the strange-looking bird collapse onto the ground by her side.

But Mulan *did* spot the bird the next day as she and Black Wind made their way along a snowy mountain pass. Her teeth chattering with cold, she hunched as close to Black Wind's neck as she could, but even the large horse provided little warmth. As they came around a bend in the pass, Mulan's eyes narrowed.

The bird was back.

Shivering so violently that the few feathers it had fell off, and with beak chattering, the bird stood in the middle of the snowy pass. It appeared to be trying to block Mulan's way. "You," Mulan said, pulling Black Wind to a halt. "What do you want?"

The bird let out a sad squawk.

Dismounting, Mulan approached the bird. Close up, the creature was even more unfortunate-looking. Mulan felt sad. The bird was sickly and pathetic. But there was also something familiar about it. And a stubbornness in the bird's eyes made it seem stronger than its molting, skinny body would suggest.

"Please," Mulan said, this time her voice gentle, "move aside."

The bird did not move.

Sighing, Mulan lifted her foot and tried to nudge the bird. To her surprise, her foot was met with resistance. For such a weak thing, the bird was surprisingly strong. Mulan pushed harder. The bird still did not move. Letting out a shout, Mulan pushed once more. This time she managed to edge the bird off the path and close to where the pass dropped off.

Mulan grabbed Black Wind's reins and led him past the bird. She looked over her shoulder and saw that the bird was still standing there, watching them go. The same odd sense of sadness washed over Mulan, and for a moment, she thought about going back for the bird. But then she shook her head. She didn't need any more baggage and she definitely didn't need a sickly bird slowing her down.

Mulan did not think she could go on. The last of her rice had run out a day before and both she and Black Wind were weakened with hunger. Leaving the mountains behind, she sat slumped in her saddle, the reins loose as she let Black Wind make his own path.

The sun was just beginning to sink toward the horizon when Mulan caught sight of a town in the distance. She sat up a little straighter, her stomach rumbling in anticipation. Relief flickered in her heart. Black Wind saw the town, too, and his footsteps quickened. By the time they approached the outskirts of the town, he was cantering and Mulan was smiling.

But her smile faded as she got off Black Wind and walked him through the new town. Every face she saw was that of a stranger. The eyes that followed her were dark and suspicious. She had never known any village but her own. She had never met strangers. Now she was surrounded by them.

Tying Black Wind to a post outside the only tavern in the town, Mulan gave him a pat. "Wish me luck," she whispered. The big horse nickered and then bumped her with his head toward the doors of the tavern. Taking a deep breath, Mulan walked inside.

The room was dark and smoky, filled with the smell of roasted meat, ale, and dirty men. Mulan kept her head down, her heart thumping loudly in her chest. Scanning the room from beneath lowered lids, she spotted a small table at the far end. She made her way over and slumped onto the chair. If she could have made herself invisible, she would have. But then she wouldn't get food.

Suddenly, the large burly innkeeper appeared next to the table, eyes cold and arms crossed over his chest. While he was an innkeeper and therefore made his living from serving strangers, he certainly didn't seem to like them. "We have noodles with pork or pork with noodles," he said with a grunt.

Mulan nodded, not trusting herself to speak.

"That a yes?" the innkeeper asked.

"Yes," Mulan said, trying to keep her voice deep and low like a man's.

The innkeeper didn't move. He kept standing there, looking down at Mulan. Mulan shrank further into her armor. She had told him what she wanted. Why wasn't he leaving? She dared another look at the big man.

"Pay before you eat," he said, holding out his hand.

Right. Money. It was an inn full of travelers. Of course the man would demand payment up front. There was just a teeny tiny problem. She didn't exactly *have* money, not in the traditional sense. Keeping her head down, she reached into her bag and pulled out a small cloth pouch. She handed it to the innkeeper.

"What is this?" he asked, looking down at the pouch, which looked even smaller in his huge hands.

"Tea," Mulan said.

The innkeeper raised one bushy eyebrow. "Well, this must be my lucky day," he said. Then, turning to the rest of the room, he called out, "The soldier wants to pay with tea!"

The room erupted in cruel laughter.

"It's all that I have," Mulan protested, knowing the excuse sounded weak.

The innkeeper shook his head. "No," he said. "You have more than that. Your sword, for instance." He nodded at the weapon resting at her side. "Your armor. I hear you have a handsome horse outside. Trade all three and you can eat like an emperor for a year."

Mulan's skin grew clammy and her heart pounded against her chest. She had thought she'd kept a low profile, but clearly this man, and the other patrons, had observed her from the moment she'd arrived. They had noted her weapons and Black Wind. She felt very, very afraid. What if they tried to rob her?

The sounds of laughter—at her expense—filled the room. Mulan looked at the faces of the strangers and saw no compassion or sympathy in any of them. The feeling of fear grew stronger. Getting to her feet, Mulan grabbed her things—and the tea—and rushed out of the tavern.

Jumping up on Black Wind's back, she urged him into a run. She would just have to wait until they got to the next town to eat. Her stomach rumbled angrily. Hopefully, it wouldn't be too far away.

EIGHT

Mulan sat in front of a fire, trying to warm her hands. The fire was small. She had not had the strength or energy to search the surrounding woods for more than a handful of twigs. But as she tried to warm up, she wished she had spent a little more time gathering firewood.

Groaning, she pulled off her father's boots. The rags she had stuffed in the shoes to help them fit better came out tinged red. Blisters, some new and some old, lined her feet, which were bloody and raw. She grimaced at the sight and then stretched them toward the fire. Reaching down, she grabbed her small food bag and looked inside. There was only one lonely apple remaining. Sighing, she offered it up to Black Wind, who devoured it.

"Maybe if I beg forgiveness, my family will take me back . . ." she said when the sound of Black Wind's chomping had grown quiet. The horse didn't respond. Looking across the fire, Mulan's eyes grew wide.

The bird was back.

The same ugly, strange bird that she had now seen three separate times sat on a nearby log, watching her. Mulan's stomach rumbled. "Is that hideous bird too ugly to eat?" she asked Black Wind.

In answer, the bird let out a loud squawk.

Mulan's stomach rumbled again. She reached for her sword. Ugly didn't necessarily mean not tasty. She was pushing herself to her feet when she heard footsteps behind her. Startled, she turned, giving the bird a chance to hop to safety.

"Greetings!"

The sound of a man's voice bounced off the trees. Wrapping her fingers around the hilt of her sword, Mulan turned, the weapon raised in front of her. Two monks, with long beards and ragged cloaks, were looking at her from across the fire. They appeared to be much older than her, their faces weathered with age. One's skin and hair were darker, while the other had a lighter complexion. Behind them was a pathetic-looking donkey.

"Be at ease, my friend," the monk with the darker hair said. "We are simply monks traveling the world, doing good deeds to ensure happiness and keep chaos at bay." The other monk nodded and flashed her a smile. Mulan's face remained stony. The dark-haired man went on, pointing at the smiling monk. "This is Brother Ramtish. I am Brother Skatch. We bring you food and fellowship."

Food? Just the word itself made Mulan's mouth water. And when the two monks brought the food out, any remaining fear vanished. Dropping her weapon, she grabbed a plate and some rice and sat down. Despite the overwhelming urge to shovel all of it in her mouth at once, she heard her mother's voice in her head, telling her to eat slowly, with grace. *But Mother was never on the verge of starving,* Mulan thought, though she did as she had been taught.

Watching her, Ramtish chuckled. Turning, he looked at Skatch. "I think he's the most polite starving person I've ever seen."

Skatch nodded. "Yes, he is a gentleman of remarkably good manners." He reached toward his bag. "Brother Ramtish, I say we celebrate this repast with a taste of wine."

Mulan stifled a smile. She had a feeling the good brothers liked to celebrate—a lot. But they had been referring to her as a man thus far, so if their celebration allowed her to remain anonymous, she would look the other way. But then Skatch poured a drink and offered it to her.

"Thank you," Mulan said, shaking her head. "But I do not drink."

"A soldier who doesn't drink?" Skatch repeated. "Brother Ramtish, there's something peculiar about our dining companion."

Mulan stopped chewing, her heartbeat quickening as both monks turned and gazed at her searchingly.

Skatch went on, "Does he look like any soldier you've ever seen?"

"He does not," Ramtish answered.

Mulan swallowed the rest of the rice that now felt like rocks in her stomach. Then, clearing her throat, she tried to explain away their doubts. "Well, technically," she began, being sure to keep her voice low, "I am not a soldier *yet*. This is my father's sword and armor." She pointed to both. "I am a conscript for the Imperial Army in the fight against the northern invaders."

Skatch's eyes narrowed but he nodded. "Yes, the northern invaders," he said, taking a deep drink from his cup. "Led by Böri Khan. We heard they were back."

"He was angry *before* they killed him," Ramtish said, taking his own drink with a chuckle. "Imagine how furious he is now?"

The two monks shared another laugh, and another drink, before Skatch returned his attention to Mulan. She had, in the meantime, scooted farther away. But the clearing was small. There wasn't much room for her to move. "So, what's your name, soldier-to-be?" Skatch asked.

"I represent the Hua family," Mulan answered.

"You don't have a first name?" Skatch probed.

Mulan frowned. It was clear the monk was not going to let this go. She ran through the boys in her village before settling on a name. "My first name is . . . Jun," she told him.

"Well, Hua Jun," Skatch said, stretching out the name, "I'm going to be honest with you. I can't see you lasting a day in the army. You're going to be eaten alive." From where he sat, Ramtish nodded in agreement. "If you're going to be a soldier, you've got to be a *man*."

Mulan's breath hitched in her throat and she hoped her cheeks weren't flushing red. "What makes you think I'm not a man?"

Skatch laughed. "You act like a boy," he answered. He mimicked her careful placement of food in her mouth. "You've got to look like a man, smell like a man, *act* like a man!"

The breath escaped her lungs in a whoosh as she realized her secret was still safe. Unaware of her thoughts, the monk began to tromp around the fire. Mulan bit back a smile. She wouldn't have been surprised if he'd pounded on his chest and yelled for effect. Still, what he was saying *was* intriguing, and something she had not given much thought to. "How *does* a man act?" she asked.

"For one thing, he doesn't eat like a woman." Once again, Skatch pretended to be her, daintily picking at a grain of rice. "Men eat like it's the last meal they'll ever have." This time, he mimed shoveling food into his face, even lapping his tongue at the air as though licking a bowl. Mulan had to stop herself from grimacing. He looked like a pig.

But that was Skatch's point: men behaved like pigs. They were also almost always confident. "You walked into that tavern tonight like you were hiding something." This time, he imitated Mulan's shrinking figure as she entered the tavern. Ramtish laughed. Skatch stopped and planted his feet, squaring his shoulders before going on. "When a real man enters a room, he *owns* that room. It's his territory. You might not announce it, but you've got to believe it." Then, to Mulan's amusement, he actually did pound his chest. "Ha!" he yelled. Then he gestured to Mulan to stand by him. "Show me."

Taking a deep breath, Mulan walked over to the monk. She planted her feet, just as he had. Then she squared her shoulders, just as he had. And finally, she pounded her chest, just as he had. "HA!" she shouted. To her ears, the word came out as a squeak.

But Skatch seemed pleased. "Yes!" he cried. "That's it! You don't go looking for trouble, but you don't back away from it, either. Especially from a snaggletoothed, foul-odored innkeeper."

His hand whipped forward, grabbing the sword out of Mulan's grasp. Before she could even blink, he had the tip of the blade pointed right below her chin. "Pay before I eat?" he said, as though he were addressing the innkeeper himself. "My payment's the tip of my blade. So, either I eat now . . . *or you die.*"

Mulan couldn't help thinking that, for a monk, he seemed remarkably capable with a weapon. Flipping the sword in his hand, Skatch held out the handle to Mulan.

"Never let someone take your sword, by the way," he said. "Very bad idea."

"Oh. Sorry—" Mulan began.

"Apologizing isn't recommended, either," Skatch said, cutting her off. "And another thing—"

This time, he was the one who was interrupted.

Letting out a loud burp, Ramtish hit his chest with his fist. "Brother Skatch," he said, "this man's trying to eat his dinner and you're blabbering on like a woman."

Skatch held his hand to his heart. "Apologies, Hua Jun," he said. "Please—let us sit. Relax. Enjoy your meal."

He turned and joined Ramtish, who had made himself quite comfortable on a fallen log. Running his hand through his dark hair, he smiled at his friend as Ramtish refilled both their cups. A few drops spilled over, staining the ground where they fell a light red.

Mulan's eyes narrowed as she watched the two men tilt back their cups and drink deeply.

"There are many paths to truth," Skatch said, in response to the judgment he saw in Mulan's eyes.

Silence settled over the small clearing as the two monks stared into the flickering flames of the fire and Mulan stared at them. She was still unsure exactly what they were doing there. They had fed her, for which she was grateful, but she had assumed they would soon be on their way. Yet they lingered.

Since they didn't appear to be going anywhere, Mulan figured she should at least make conversation. "You said there was another thing."

"Pardon?" Skatch said, looking up from his cup. His eyes already seemed a little glazed and his voice less clear.

"You know," Mulan prompted. "About being a man. Another thing I should know?"

Skatch frowned, and Ramtish nudged him. The pair shared a look that Mulan couldn't quite read before Ramtish said, "Oh, go on. You might as well tell him now."

For a moment, Skatch hesitated, and Mulan wondered if he was going to heed his friend's advice or ignore him. Mulan felt a flash of impatience, but then he nodded. "Here's the most fundamental thing of all." Skatch paused, his eyes locking with Mulan's and all traces of his fogginess disappearing. "A real man never refuses a drink."

As Skatch finished his "lesson," Ramtish casually placed a cup of wine in front of Mulan. She looked down at the red liquid, then up at the monks, and then back down at the wine. She had never tasted a drop of the liquid in her life. Even at the few celebrations she had attended in her village, her mother had strictly forbidden it, telling Mulan it would make her act unladylike. But now she didn't have a choice. If she refused, the monks would figure out her secret.

So, taking a deep breath, she grabbed the cup, brought it to her lips . . . and drank the contents down in one long gulp.

Skatch looked down at the young soldier, who was now lying beside the fire. He was out cold. The liquid had done its trick. The moment he had spotted the young man, Skatch had known he would be an easy mark. The boy reeked of innocence and naiveté. All it had taken was the one glass of wine and Hua Jun had passed out. Now he lay there, half his face covered in dirt, oblivious to the movement around him.

Lifting a hand, Skatch rubbed his now hairless chin. The fake beard he had been wearing was hanging underneath his chin, giving his skin a chance to feel the fresh air. Turning, he saw Ramtish strapping the warrior's sword to the back of the horse's saddle. The huge animal shifted on his feet, clearly aware that something strange was going on.

"We have the horse and the sword," Ramtish said, giving the rope around the sword one final tug to make sure it was secure. He nodded at the warrior on the ground. "Let's strip him and take his armor."

Not waiting for Skatch's permission, Ramtish leaned down and reached to unlace the young warrior's armor. But before he could finish, a loud, ugly bird appeared out of nowhere. Ramtish swung his arms around, trying to keep the bird at bay. But the creature kept coming, its eyes wild and sparse feathers flying. With a shout, he managed to swat the bird, sending it soaring.

But it doubled back immediately, attacking again. This time, Ramtish didn't bother with his hand. Instead, he reached down and unsheathed his own sword. It whooshed through the air as he brought it up, the tip pointing directly at the oncoming bird.

This time, the bird stopped.

"Brother?" Skatch asked, watching the interaction with a mixture of curiosity and amusement. He wasn't sure why the bird seemed so protective of the warrior, but it was clear the creature wanted Ramtish nowhere near him. "Leave his armor. And the sword."

Ramtish looked over, surprise on his face. "What?" he said. He and Skatch had been working together for years. Never once, in all that time, had Skatch left something of value behind when there was something of value to be had.

"There's something about this young man I like," Skatch said, shrugging. His eyes lingered on the warrior. In sleep, the young man looked even more innocent. "He's an underdog, like ourselves," he added.

"Speak for yourself," Ramtish retorted. "As dogs go, I prefer to think of myself as a champion."

Skatch laughed as he hooked his fake beard around his ears and pushed it back into place. "Leave him the donkey, too," Skatch added. "Since I am in a very generous mood." Then, grabbing the horse's reins, he led the big animal out of the clearing. Ramtish took one last longing look at the armor and weapon and then, with a sigh, followed.

Behind them, the warrior lay, his breath heavy, his eyes still closed.

NINE

I'm dead, Mulan thought. *That is why I feel so terrible. I've died and I'm being eternally punished because I disobeyed my family.*

Mulan opened her eyes and immediately shut them again. She wasn't dead, but she almost wished she were, because then maybe she wouldn't feel so awful. Her head was pounding and her cheeks felt as though they were on fire. She tried to move an arm to cover her face from the relentless sun above, but her arms felt too heavy to lift.

She stopped moving and simply lay for a moment, yelling at herself and the monks for making her feel this way. She should never have listened to Skatch's "advice." A smart warrior would *not* drink wine. Especially if this was how they felt after.

Something pecked her nose. "Ouch!" Mulan shouted, her eyes snapping open. To her surprise—and annoyance—the ugly bird was staring down at her. Mulan frowned when she realized the bird was scowling at her, as though judging her current state.

Sitting up quickly, Mulan instantly regretted her choice. The movement made her head pound even harder. She let out a moan. Then, when she could stomach it, she looked around, eager to tell Skatch and Ramtish just what she thought about their advice.

Her stomach heaved.

The fire was out. The monks were gone—and so was Black Wind!

In a flash, Mulan was on her feet. The clearing was silent. Whistling loudly, she waited. There was no answering whicker or sound of hoof beats. She whistled again. Still nothing. Mulan's heart dropped as her greatest fear was realized. Black Wind was gone.

In his place was the monks' raggedy, tired donkey.

Mulan bit back a scream. She had no horse and no food. Stomping her foot in frustration, she yelped as she realized that her shoes were gone, too! And she hadn't even reached the army yet.

Taking a deep breath, Mulan steadied her racing heart. She had come this far. She wasn't going to turn back now. She owed it to her family—and herself. Gathering her few remaining possessions, she brushed her fingers over the writing on the smooth metal of her father's sword. LOYAL. BRAVE. TRUE. The words had gotten her father through his own battle and were now a part of her story, for better or worse.

Strapping the sword to her back, she grabbed the reins of the donkey and led it out of the clearing. The donkey's steps were slow and plodding, and every few feet the stubborn animal tried to stop to grab a piece of grass. Mulan tugged impatiently at the reins. *Could anything else go wrong?* she wondered.

As if in answer, she heard a loud squawk.

Looking up, she saw the ugly bird once again standing in her way. The creature's wings were spread, its head tilted to the side as it stared back at her. *That is it!* Mulan fumed silently. *First the monks, now this bird again. Enough is enough!*

"You!" she shouted. "Leave me alone!"

The bird didn't move—at first. Then, as Mulan watched, it shifted on its feet. Bringing its wings behind it, the bird stretched out its neck as if in mid-flight. Mulan gasped as she began to recognize the elongated neck, open wings, and powerful stance. Could it be?

"The phoenix statue?" Mulan ventured, seeing the creature for what it was: the bird from her family's shrine brought to life.

The Phoenix dropped her wings and nodded, as if to say, *Finally!*

"What?" Mulan said, trying to make sense of the situation. Her father had told her the bird was meant to watch over her. But she had thought he meant metaphorically. "You're here to *protect* me?" She eyed the bird, who gave a barely perceptible nod. Mulan wanted to laugh. And cry. This had to be a joke. A cruel joke. How could a bird with barely enough feathers to protect its own body help her? "Couldn't I just have my horse back?" she asked.

In response, the Phoenix let out a very un-birdlike hiss. She hopped over toward Mulan, then moved past her and jumped on the back of the donkey. Settling in, she made herself comfortable, ignoring the daggers Mulan was shooting at her with her eyes.

"You can get as comfortable as you like," Mulan said. "But I'm not going home."

The Phoenix didn't move. But the judgment in her eyes lessened.

"I'm going to fight for my country," Mulan said, unsure why she felt the need to defend herself to the Phoenix. The bird's expression did not change. "I don't need you," Mulan added.

This time, the Phoenix shrugged, her thoughts as clear as if she had said them aloud. *Time will tell*, her look said. *Time will tell*. Then, with one last squawk, the Phoenix shifted again on the donkey's back so that she was facing his tail. Sitting down, she settled in, clearly ready to enjoy the ride.

Mulan sighed. It looked like the Phoenix was tagging along, whether Mulan needed her or not. Grabbing the reins, Mulan tugged the donkey forward. She was going to make quite the spectacle walking into the army's encampment with a donkey and a phoenix that looked like a plucked chicken.

But that was a problem she would face when she came to it. First, she just needed to *get* to the encampment.

While Mulan's journey had felt like it would never end, it finally did.

As they arrived at the edge of a huge field, her eyes grew wide as she took in the sights and sounds of the huge army encampment. Banners flew above large tents surrounded by smaller ones. The smell of cooking food wafted through the air, making Mulan's stomach rumble once again. The sounds of horses' hooves blended with clanging metal as soldiers practiced fighting. Large gates had been set up on the outskirts of the camp. In front of them was a line of hundreds of men, all clutching conscription papers. Every few minutes, a dozen or so would be ushered through the gates and disappear inside the teeming encampment. Mulan watched, trying to make sense of the bustling scene in front of her. It was like nothing she had seen before. Her eyes lingered on the future soldiers, each waiting their turn. Some were young, their faces eager, others old, their faces wise and drawn. But they were all men.

Taking a deep breath, Mulan pulled the donkey forward. The Phoenix, who had fallen asleep shortly into the ride, woke with a start. Seeing the encampment, she let out a squawk and jumped off the donkey, hopping over to some bushes for cover. For the briefest of moments, Mulan thought about following her. But then she remembered the words on the sword. *Brave. Loyal. True.* She had to be brave now.

Throwing back her shoulders, Mulan strode forward, silently thanking—and cursing—the monks for their "lesson." She took her place in line. Ahead of her were two young men, roughly her age. One was chubby, his cheeks flushed. He looked awkward and uncomfortable, and Mulan couldn't help feeling a wave of empathy. She imagined her own cheeks were red, too—if not from embarrassment, then from the many hours she had spent traveling in the sun. Beside him was a taller conscript. He said something to the larger boy and then laughed, revealing a sizable gap between his two front teeth that made him instantly look younger. Mulan stood quietly behind them, trying not to eavesdrop.

Just then, another young man, older by a few years it would seem, cut in front of her. Ignoring her grunt of protest, he stopped inches behind the two boys. A long weed hung from the side of his mouth. Taking it out, he tickled the larger boy's ear.

"I'm Cricket," the boy was saying.

"Longwei," the other conscript said, introducing himself.

Cricket nodded. "My mother said I was born—" He stopped, lifting his hand to swat away the "insect" that was tickling his ear.

Behind him, the older conscript bit back a laugh. Another conscript joined him, pointing to the weed and miming for him to do it again. Mulan watched them with narrowed eyes. Cricket had done nothing to them. What was the point of teasing him in such a way?

Unaware of the situation, Cricket continued chatting. His voice was friendly and open. "She said I was born under an auspicious—" The tickling had grown more aggressive and Cricket swatted harder this time. Only, instead of slapping a bug, he accidently slapped Longwei.

"Ow!" he shouted, putting a hand to his cheek.

Behind them, the two bullies howled with laughter. Then, pushing Cricket and Longwei out of the way, they took their place in line. The younger conscripts stumbled against each other, trying to keep their balance.

Sensing she was about to get tumbled into, Mulan moved out of the way. But she hadn't seen the conscript who had come up beside her. With a shout, she crashed into him, the impact knocking her to the ground.

She lay still for a moment, trying to catch her breath. Then she saw a hand held out to her.

"Sorry, tadpole," the conscript said. "My mistake."

Mulan tried to keep herself from blushing. The young man in front of her was tall, lean, and very, *very* handsome. His eyes were twinkling and kind.

He offered his hand again.

Distracted by his good looks and the charming smile he was flashing at her, Mulan almost, *almost* took his hand. But then she stopped. *Tadpole* he had called her. Embarrassment, delayed, came rushing over her. This was exactly what Skatch had said would happen. She wouldn't be taken seriously.

Ignoring the outstretched hand, Mulan scrambled to her feet. Then she reached for her sword. But her hands were clammy and her fingers shaking, so what she had hoped would be a quick grab turned into a bumbling attempt to pull the sword from its belt. She pulled it free and, lifting it in the air, pointed it at the other conscript's throat just as Skatch had done to her. "Insult me again," she said, forcing her voice to go deep, "and you'll taste the tip of my blade!"

Instantly, all humor left the young man's face. Before she even heard the swish of his sword, she felt its tip at her own throat. Mulan gulped. She *might* have been a bit hasty in her actions. Skatch hadn't told her what to do if the other person also had a weapon.

"Lower your sword," the conscript said.

"Or *what*?" Mulan had been trying for tough, but even to her, her voice sounded flimsy.

Mulan felt Cricket's and Longwei's eyes on her, as well as the bullies'. She could sense them looking back and forth between her and the young man across from her. She heard someone whisper "Honghui," and a few others repeat the name. Her arm shook and she wanted to drop her sword, but she couldn't. Not until the other conscript, or rather Honghui, dropped his.

Out of the corner of her eye, she saw another person approaching. It was an older man, his face lined with age and experience. There was a flash of movement. Before Mulan could blink, her arm was twisted behind her back. A moment later the sword was removed from her hand and her arm dropped to her side. Next to her, Honghui rubbed his own arm, his eyes on his weapon.

"I am your commanding officer—Commander Tung!" the man shouted. "Fighting will not be tolerated. Am I clear?" He stared at the young man, his eyes icy.

"Yes, Commander," the other conscript said immediately.

The commander turned to Mulan and repeated the question. Mulan's voice stuck in her throat. She nodded.

"With your voice, soldier," Commander Tung ordered.

"Yes, Commander," Mulan said.

Across from her, Honghui took back his sword and glared at Mulan. She had messed up. Already she was gaining enemies, not allies.

Handing Mulan her sword, the commander hesitated, his gaze catching on the engraving on its blade. Recognition flashed over his face and he looked up at Mulan with renewed interest. "What's your name, soldier?" he asked.

"Hua Jun, Commander," Mulan said, the fib gliding off her tongue.

"Is this your family's sword?" Commander Tung asked.

Mulan nodded and then remembered that the commander wanted words. "It belongs to my father, Hua Zhou," she said.

There was a moment as the commander looked back and forth between the sword and Mulan, his face still but his eyes flickering with emotion. Then, noticing her bare feet, he nodded toward a tent behind them. "Go get yourself a pair of boots," he said. Before Mulan could respond, Commander Tung had marched off, disappearing into the hustle and bustle of the encampment.

Mulan watched him go. When he was out of

sight, she let out the breath she had been holding. The commander could have had her punished or sent her away. Instead, he had seemed to take an interest in her—or at least her family name. While she wasn't thrilled that she already had enemies among the other conscripts, the encounter at least meant she was getting boots. Which, she thought, looking down at her bloody feet, couldn't have come at a better time.

Mulan gathered her things and headed toward the clothing tent. The more distance she could get from Honghui, the better. In another world and another setting, Mulan had a feeling Cricket would've been a friend. But she wasn't going to stick around to find out if her hunch was right. She would get her boots, and then she would think about the mess she had gotten herself into. She had been so worried about surviving the war that she hadn't even thought about surviving boot camp.

TEN

By the time Mulan found a pair of boots that fit and training clothes that were only two sizes too big, it was growing dark. Walking out of the clothing tent, she searched for her assigned barracks. Each tent looked the same, and for a while, she wandered through the encampment, happy for the darkness and the solitude. After weeks of being alone, she realized she had grown used to the solitary sounds of the thoughts in her head and Black Wind's hooves hitting the ground.

As she moved among the tents, she wrinkled her nose at the odd scents that filled the air. There was a distinct mixture of sweat, unwashed clothes, and undercooked meat. Even though she was hungry, the smell did little to entice her to fill her belly, instead making her queasy. Fires had been lit in front of the bigger tents, and soldiers stood around them, warming their hands, their booming voices all the louder in the stillness of the night.

Mulan sighed. She wanted desperately, in that moment, to be back in her family's house, sitting with her sister. She wouldn't even have protested if her mother tried to play with her unruly hair, twisting it and looping it as she mumbled to herself. *Your hair is like you, Mulan, impossible to control,* she would say. But her voice would be soft, and Mulan would feel her mother's gentle fingers brush over her shoulders, silently adding, *I love you.*

Shaking her head, Mulan pushed away the thoughts of home. They would do her no good. The monks had told her she had to act like a man. And men didn't get weepy and sentimental. Spotting her assigned tent, Mulan slipped inside.

Immediately, she wished she hadn't.

In front of her, men in various stages of undress joked and laughed with one another. Mulan's face flushed and she felt her throat become dry. Two of the conscripts were trading playful punches while they argued over who should get the better sleeping platform. Another conscript was searching through his clothing, tossing things over his shoulder without care. There was a conscript sharpening his sword and another picking his teeth with the tip of a dagger.

Keeping her eyes down, Mulan made her way through the tent. Other than the soldiers, the tent itself was practically empty. The only furniture was the eight sleeping platforms that ran the length of the tent. Beside most of them were piles of clothing and equipment, thrown down by whatever soldier had claimed that platform. Spotting one of the last empty platforms, Mulan started toward it. But just as she was about to reach it, a conscript moved in front of her, his bare skin brushing Mulan's fingertips.

Mulan stopped in her tracks.

A moment later, someone bumped into her.

Turning, Mulan bit back a groan. It was Cricket. And with him was Longwei. They returned her gaze, eyebrows raised. But before any of them could speak, the larger conscript that had been bullying them earlier appeared. He, like almost everyone else, was nearly naked. As he spotted the younger conscripts, a huge smile spread over his face. For a moment, it almost looked as though he were genuinely happy to see Cricket and Longwei, like they were long-lost friends. But then he grabbed them both in a headlock and pulled them into the growing ruckus caused by the rowdy conscripts.

Desperate to get as far from the chaos as she could, Mulan once again tried to get to the empty sleeping platform. But it seemed fate was not on her side, for just as she reached it, her eyes moved up and locked on Honghui. The handsome conscript was standing next to his friend, a man Mulan recalled another conscript calling Po.

"Look who's here," Po said, nudging Honghui.

For a moment, Mulan had a flash of hope that maybe Honghui would have forgotten about their earlier interaction and be ready to move on.

But then the conscript looked over at her. His expression darkened.

Or not, Mulan thought. She knew that if Skatch and Ramtish had been there they would've told her that a true man did not apologize. But the last thing Mulan needed was an enemy. The less attention she had on her, the better. With that in mind, she opened her mouth to apologize, but before she could, a loud voice boomed through the tent. Instantly, the conscripts stopped their roughhousing as all eyes turned toward the front entrance. Sergeant Qiang, their commanding officer, stood with his face in shadow.

"I told you to line up for showers!" he said, his tone angry.

"Showers?" Mulan repeated, panic flooding through her.

Sergeant Qiang nodded. "Showers! You lot stink!"

As the other conscripts filed out, ready to follow orders and eager to wash the stink off themselves, Mulan stood and fiddled with her armor. She couldn't take a shower. Her secret would be out and she would be in serious trouble.

But she would also be in trouble if she refused an order. She nervously played with her new shirt, picking at a loose hem. She had no choice. She was just going to have to run away. Take her things and hightail it back home and suffer the consequences. There was nothing else she could do. . . .

"And I need a volunteer for night guard duty—"

Mulan didn't hesitate. Her hand shot up in the air. "Me!" she said. Her voice was loud and she sounded way too eager for the mundane task. Lowering her hand she added, this time more calmly, "I mean, I volunteer, sir." As she made her way over to the sergeant, she saw Honghui and Po share a look.

"Better keep an eye out," Honghui warned, though he didn't sound very concerned.

Po nodded. "Those northern invaders *eat* tadpoles," he added.

As he pushed past her, Po opened his mouth and bit at the air. Mulan kept her expression neutral. She wouldn't give them the satisfaction of seeing her rattled. But as soon as they were gone, she shivered. Joking aside, she had just volunteered for a job that put her on the first line of defense against the invaders.

If the sergeant hadn't been standing there waiting, Mulan would have hit herself upside the head. She just kept getting herself into deeper—and hotter—water. Then her lips formed into a rueful smile at the irony of her thought. She wasn't getting into any water—just trouble.

Mulan stood, chilled to the bone, as she stared out into the darkness beyond the barrack walls. As the only conscript on the tower, she had been told, or rather ordered, to keep her eyes peeled and her ears open. The invaders, the sergeant had been happy to tell her, would be able to see her before she could see them. And if they got through the gates on her watch, they would be the least of her worries.

For the first few hours, Mulan had actually enjoyed the patrol. The guard tower was quiet, and for the first time since she had arrived at the camp, she had been able to relax. Her breath had become even, her heartbeat returning to normal after what had felt like constant galloping, and she had even, a few times, hummed to herself in her regular voice. But about three hours in, it started to get cold, and an hour later, the clouds rolled in. By the time she was only halfway through her shift, rain was falling in sheets in front of her.

But not *on* her.

The realization startled her, and she looked up. She groaned as she saw the Phoenix. The bird was perched on the edge of the roof of the guard tower, her wing outstretched, creating an umbrella for Mulan. Mulan's eyes narrowed. She had told the bird to leave her alone. The last thing she needed was to have someone spot her being taken care of by a large, ugly bird.

She took a wide step to the right. Instantly, she was drenched.

Up on the roof, the bird shuffled to the right. The rain stopped.

Growing angry, Mulan stepped in the opposite direction. As rain covered her face and soaked her clothes, she looked up at the Phoenix. "I told you," she hissed. "I don't need you."

The Phoenix shrugged, as if to say, *Fine, be that way*, and then deliberately folded in her wings. Mulan was left to stand in the rain.

Mulan's eyes drooped and her body shivered from a combination of cold and exhaustion by the time the next conscript arrived to relieve her. Not trusting her own voice, Mulan nodded to him and then hastily made her way back to her barracks. All she wanted to do was lie down and sleep.

But when she pushed back the flap on the tent, her dreams of getting a good night's rest faded. Every platform was taken. Some of the sleeping berths even had more than one conscript lying across them. Loud snores and an occasional grunt sounded through the tent, making it almost as loud as if everyone were up and talking. Taking a deep breath, Mulan tiptoed down the narrow lane between the platforms. Her eyes scanned left to right and back again, desperately looking for an empty space. She passed Honghui and Po, lying back to back. She briefly thought about wringing out her wet shirt over their heads to get back at them for the tadpole comment, but thought better of it when Honghui grunted loudly. Even in sleep he was intimidating.

Just as she was about to give up and go find a place to sleep outside, she spotted a tiny, narrow space at the very end of the tent. She made her way over. Looking around to make sure that no one had awoken, she took off the wettest and dirtiest of her layers. She winced as she lifted them over her head. Her shoulders were stiff from hours of standing still, and she dreaded to think what they would feel like tomorrow. But as she pulled at the tight leather bindings that covered her chest, she took a grateful gulp of air. The bindings were necessary to protect her identity, but they were not comfortable.

Dressed in a simple long white shirt that she hoped hid most of her curves, Mulan carefully lay down. For one glorious moment, she simply relaxed there with her eyes closed, letting her muscles take a break.

And then the soldier beside her let out a loud snort and turned over. As he did so, he threw his arm across Mulan, pinning her down. To her horror, she realized it wasn't just any conscript—it was Yao! The same guy who had bullied Cricket. Lifting a hand, she tried to gingerly move his arm off, but then he let out another snort and flung his other hand across her. Now not only was her body pinned down, but her arms were, too. She was trapped.

Mulan's mind raced while her body remained frozen. She had to get Yao off her. But how? She couldn't move her arms and she definitely couldn't afford to wake him up and have him see her without her armor on. The white shirt was good enough camouflage for a distant onlooker, but Yao was way too close for comfort—on many levels.

Out of the corner of her eye she saw a feather appear. It was scrawny and faded but as she watched, it began to tickle Yao's nose. Ever so carefully, she lifted her head. The Phoenix was standing at the edge of the platform, using her tail feathers to tickle Yao. He mumbled in his sleep and tried to brush away the feather, but the Phoenix kept tickling. Yao sneezed. Half waking himself in the process, he flipped over, turning his back to Mulan and throwing an arm around the soldier on the other side.

Mulan exhaled. Looking over at the bird, who was starting to hop out of the tent, Mulan gave her a reluctant nod. Maybe she did need her . . . a little bit.

ELEVEN

"**S**tealing! Penalty: death!"

Sergeant Qiang's voice rang over the parade ground in the center of the encampment. Morning had come far too quickly for Mulan's liking. She had been awakened by the sergeant's loud voice billowing through the tent, ordering everyone outside for the morning announcements. Luckily, in the rush that had followed, Mulan had been able to slink into the shadows of the tent and dress. Now she stood shoulder to shoulder with hundreds of other conscripts and seasoned soldiers as the sergeant barked a list of rules and the punishments for breaking them. Beside him, Commander Tung stood, his eyes moving over the men gathered in front of him.

"Desertion!" Sergeant Qiang went on. "Penalty: death!"

The men listened, their faces somber. Even Yao knew not to joke.

"Bringing women into camp or consorting with women in any way," the sergeant continued. "Penalty: death!"

Mulan struggled to keep the panic and fear from her face. She felt as though everyone was looking at her, though she knew that was not the case. Still, hearing Sergeant Qiang's words made her fears feel that much more real. She had known there was a penalty for women in the army, but death? That seemed a bit . . . aggressive.

As if reading her thoughts, Sergeant Qiang finished his speech. "Dishonesty? Penalty . . ." He paused, letting the word hang in the air for a moment before finishing. "Expulsion! Disgrace."

The conscripts gasped.

Sergeant Qiang nodded. "Disgrace for you, disgrace for your family, disgrace for your village . . . disgrace for your country."

From the looks on the faces of the men around her, and from the way they all shifted uncomfortably on their feet, Mulan knew they were thinking the same thing she was thinking. Disgrace was a far worse punishment than death.

Mulan could have sworn Sergeant Qiang looked happier to have made all the soldiers nervous. Marching in front of them, he stopped, slamming his finger into the chest of the nearest conscript. "We're going to make men out of every single one of you!"

As the parade ground erupted with cheers, Mulan halfheartedly lifted her own hand and voice. But on the inside, she shrank. How could they make a man out of her when she wasn't a man to begin with? And worse still, what would her future look like if anyone ever found out the truth?

Mulan was exhausted. After their morning "talking to," they had been sent out into the middle of the parade grounds to begin their basic training. For hours, she and the other "men" had been practicing the same basic martial arts maneuvers over and over again. Using only their arms, legs, and body weight, they were supposed to defend themselves with minimal effort. Mulan's arms hurt from swinging through the air, and she was sure she had heard a loud pop in her hip during one overzealous kick. But she didn't let the pain stop her. As other soldiers fell to the ground in exhaustion, Mulan kept going. She felt the eyes of Commander Tung on her and it drove her on. At one point, she was certain her body had gone numb, and her limbs moved as if pulled by strings. It reminded her of being in the village, weaving on the loom, the actions becoming so routine that her mind could wander.

Only now, she couldn't afford to let her thoughts drift from the task at hand. Slipping up, she heard Sergeant Qiang shout at her and hastily redid the move, fixing her mistake. Satisfied, the sergeant moved on to torturing the next conscript in line, Honghui.

Mulan snuck a peek at him. Despite the hard work, his moves were fresh, his face still focused.

Cricket and Longwei were not faring as well. Both were panting, their faces red and sweat pouring from their brows. A competitive wave washed over and she felt fresh energy infuse her aching body. She wasn't going to let Honghui beat her. Not mentally *or* physically.

As the day progressed, the conscripts were moved from one part of the camp to another. They spent time on the archery range, shooting arrows at a line of wicker targets set up on a hill. At the sergeant's order, the soldiers would notch their arrows and raise their bows. Then they would let the arrows fly. Mulan focused, her eyes locked on the target. But it didn't seem to matter. Each time her arrow was sent flying, it came up short. Luckily, the others seemed to be having trouble, too. Honghui's arrows flew wide while Po kept breaking the bowstring. Only Cricket, ironically enough, had any luck. Pulling back his arrow, he held it awkwardly in front of him. Mulan could see his hand shaking from the effort of keeping the bow steady. Then he closed his eyes and let the arrow loose. It zipped across the field and with a loud *THWAP!* struck the target right in the center. As she caught Honghui's eye and they traded impressed looks, Mulan felt a brief flicker of hope. Maybe she wouldn't be an outsider forever.

Their training continued into that night and the days that followed. Still avoiding showering with the other soldiers, Mulan kept volunteering for night watch, pushing her past the brink of exhaustion. But there was no reprieve. As soon as they learned how to move their limbs in the series of martial arts maneuvers, they were given their swords and required to learn the moves all over again. They continued to work on the archery field, the sun beating down on their backs as arrows flew left, right, and occasionally straight. But that was not the worst of it.

The worst was the shrine. Day after day, when the sun was highest in the sky and the hottest on their shoulders, the conscripts were given two buckets of water. Lifting the heavy, awkward vessels out until their arms were level with their shoulders, they were told to climb. The shrine, a huge structure situated on the top of a rocky cliff, was only accessible by hundreds of narrow stone steps.

Taking a deep breath, Mulan began the trek. The first few steps were manageable. But as she continued upward, her arms started to shake. Beside her and in front of her, the strongest of men began to stumble, failing at the challenge. Water sloshed over the edge of her bucket and she felt her legs growing weaker and weaker until, at last, she sank to the ground, defeated. Up ahead of her, Honghui, who had made it farther than anyone, gave up, too. Mulan stayed still, trying to catch her breath, furious at herself and her weakness.

Hearing a shout from Sergeant Qiang, she saw that the others had dumped their buckets and were making their way back down the few steps they had climbed. As they arrived at the base of the steps, the soldiers rushed toward a large trough of water. They pushed each other out of the way, thirsty and impatient. Mulan approached slowly. Waiting until the others had finished, she stepped forward. Taking the ladle, she drank.

As the water hit her lips, Mulan bit back a groan of pleasure. Her eyes closed, she didn't notice Commander Tung watching her. In the middle of the chaos, she was composed. His eyes narrowed with interest. Hua Jun was a surprise. Every task thrown at him, he had met with a quiet grace. He

Mulan is a vibrant young woman who lives in a small Chinese village.

After getting dressed up, Mulan feels out of place as she tries to impress the village matchmaker.

Hua Zhou, Mulan's father, tells her to learn her place.

Mulan holds up her father's sword.

Mulan steals her father's armor and takes off to join the army in his place.

The new conscripts wait to enter the military camp.

Mulan and the other soldiers train for battle.

The conscripts describe their ideal women during dinner.

Mulan befriends a man named Honghui.

Honghui and the other soldiers spar with practice spears.

Mulan is reunited with her horse, Black Wind, after he was stolen.

The Imperial Army charges into battle against Böri Khan's warriors.

Mulan rejoins the fight without her disguise.

Mulan goes to the Imperial City to rescue the Emperor.

The Emperor honors Mulan after she saves him from Böri Khan.

had not once complained, and even when he had been overwhelmed and weak, he had forged on. And now he had waited while the other men acted like beasts, allowing them the chance to satisfy their thirst first. Only the strongest of leaders had the strength of character to wait in such a way. The commander nodded to himself. Hua Jun was someone to keep an eye on.

"Now *she* is a girl worth fighting for."

Cricket's voice carried over the eating area. Entering the chaotic room, Mulan scanned the soldiers and seats, looking for a safe place to sit. Out of the corner of her eye, she spotted Longwei leaving their barracks, head down with his meager possessions grasped to his chest. She swallowed. She had heard his name called after the shrine. Sergeant Qiang had spotted him dumping water from his buckets to make the climb easier and immediately expelled him. It had been the smallest of infractions, but the penalty had been quick and severe. Mulan shuddered to think what would happen if her secret came to light.

Shaking her head, she returned her attention

to finding a seat. Seeing the only option was near Cricket and another young conscript named Ling, Mulan walked over and took a seat, trying not to draw attention to herself. As she started to eat, Ling held up a piece of paper. On it was a drawing of a young woman.

"We were matched twenty-seven days ago," he said to Cricket. "Her name is Li Li. Her skin is white as milk. Her fingers are like the tender white roots of a green onion. . . ."

Mulan bit back a laugh. A green onion? She wondered what this Li Li would think if she heard such a comparison.

"Ling is a romantic!" Cricket said, apparently more impressed than Mulan at Ling's choice of words.

Ling smiled dreamily. "Li Li inspires me," he went on. "Her eyes are like morning dewdrops, her hair like distant mountains, darkened by black clouds—"

Just when Mulan thought she couldn't take another simile, Yao banged his hand on the table, interrupting Ling. "I like my women buxom!" he said, letting out a loud, booming laugh. Around him, other soldiers voiced their agreement. "With strong, wide hips!" he added.

Mulan cringed. *Is this the way men talk about women?* The thought made her stomach, which had already soured at the first taste of the awful food provided, turn over. It had never occurred to her that men would have such little respect for their future wives. She had always been taught to think highly and speak proudly of the man she would someday marry. Of all men, really. Yet here, only the "romantic" seemed to have the courtesy to speak kindly of the opposite sex. Even Cricket, whom Mulan had thought was a decent man, was now taking part.

"I like kissing women with cherry red lips," he said, smiling at the men around him in the hopes of getting the same reaction Yao had received.

"Then your mother must have cherry red lips," Yao teased, "because she's the only woman that's ever kissed you!" The other soldiers snickered and Yao's smile grew broader.

"I don't care what she looks like—" Po started to say.

Thinking that the other soldier was defending

women and was going to say something nice, Mulan shot up. "I agree!" she said.

But Po's next words made her instantly regret her action. "I just care what she *cooks* like!"

Mulan's face fell. Turning her attention back to her unappetizing meal, she was surprised when she heard her name. "Tell us, Hua Jun," Honghui said, calling out to her from across the table. He had been watching her, trying to read her reaction to the room and the comments. Deciding to push her, he went on. "Tell us. What's *your* ideal woman?"

Once again, the room filled with noise as the other soldiers voiced their encouragement. "Yes!" they shouted. "Tell us!"

Mulan was mortified. She met Honghui's probing gaze and her eyes narrowed. She knew what he was trying to do. He was trying to get a rise out of her. But she wouldn't let him. She paused, collecting her thoughts before answering. "I guess," she said, making sure to keep her voice deep and steady, "my ideal woman is courageous."

The room grew silent. The men looked at each other, confused. They were all dumbfounded and disappointed. Except Honghui. He seemed interested by the answer.

Stubbornly, Mulan went on, knowing that even as she did, she was once again making herself stand out. But she didn't care. She wanted to show them that women were more than just objects. "And she has a sense of humor." Some of the men laughed. "She's also smart!" Now everyone was laughing. Everyone except Honghui.

"But what's she look like?" Cricket pressed.

Mulan shook her head. "That's not the point."

"Courageous, funny, smart," Yao repeated. "Hua Jun's not describing a woman, he's describing a *man*! He's describing me!"

As the room erupted in laughter, Mulan sank back down in her seat. What was the point? It was like trying to talk to a bunch of animals. But as she lifted her head, she was surprised to see Honghui smiling at her. He winked. Then, turning to Yao, he called out, "Courageous, funny, smart? No, that's not you, Yao. That's *definitely* not you."

The joke was now at Yao's expense, and the attention drifted from Mulan. Taking the opportunity, she slipped away. But not before giving Honghui a small, grateful smile.

TWELVE

The barracks were, for once, quiet. Mulan sat on the edge of her sleeping platform, pulling on her boots. The smallest of efforts made her muscles scream in agony and she longed to go let the hot water of the showers wash over her body. But she had volunteered for night duty again. She had no choice.

She was lacing up her boot when she heard the front flap of the barracks swish open. Looking up, she saw Honghui enter. Spotting her, he smiled broadly. Mulan forgot her sore muscles as her heart began to beat a little faster. There was something decidedly charming about Honghui, which made her uncomfortable. She was unsure why he was here now. Was she supposed to thank him for earlier? When he had come to her aid? She wasn't sure what a "man" would do in such a situation.

Luckily, she was saved from making that decision as Honghui walked over and threw himself down on the sleeping platform beside her. "Don't let them bother you," he said, putting his arms behind his head. "Especially that donkey Yao."

Mulan allowed herself a small smile. Somehow, and she wasn't quite sure how, she and Honghui had gone from being enemies to being . . . allies. Well, almost. Her thoughts drifted back to Yao's ridiculous comments in the dining hall. She still couldn't believe that he could view women as such objects, to be valued only for their physical appearance and not for their strength of character. A thought occurred to her. Honghui had never given his idea of what a "perfect" woman was. She wondered why he had been so quiet.

"Are you matched?" Honghui asked, breaking into her thoughts. "Can I ask?"

The question startled Mulan. "No," she said reflexively. But then she realized that being matched in Honghui's mind would make her seem more "manly." So she corrected herself. "I mean, yes. I was. Almost. It didn't work out."

"Lucky you," Honghui said, his voice quiet.

They sat there for a moment, his answer hanging in the air. Mulan wasn't sure what to say. Did Honghui mean she was lucky for having been matched, or for getting out of the match?

"I'm matched," Honghui said, answering her unasked question. "And I'm hoping she's courageous. And funny, and smart." He paused and his eyes grew distant. Mulan wondered, as she looked at him, what he was picturing. Then he added, "Because she looks like a man."

Honghui's admission surprised Mulan. Why would he admit this to her? What did he expect her to say? And she couldn't help wondering what he would think of her—if he could truly see her. Luckily, Honghui was too caught up in his own thoughts to notice her expression.

"I mean," he went on, "how do you even begin

to know how to *talk* to a woman, let alone be married to one?" For the first time since they had met, Honghui seemed unsure of himself. Mulan's heart, which had already begun to thaw toward the handsome conscript, grew warmer still.

Taking a chance, Mulan answered, "Just talk to her like you're talking to me now."

"I wish it was that easy," Honghui said. He paused, and his expression grew more uncertain. "What . . . what if she doesn't like me?"

Once again, his response surprised Mulan. She turned and, for the first time, really took the time to look at him. His eyes were focused on the barrack ceiling, his chest rising and falling in slow, even breaths. But Mulan could see that he was genuinely worried. In being honest, he was allowing himself to be vulnerable.

"She will," Mulan said, the words softer than she had intended.

Slowly, Honghui looked over. Their eyes met and for a hushed moment, neither said anything, the air growing heavy with unspoken emotion.

Shaking it off, Mulan cleared her throat. She had no idea what had just happened, but she *knew* she needed to lighten things up. "I mean, I think she will," she said, this time making sure to keep any emotion out of her voice. "You never know with women . . ." she added with a shrug and a conspiratorial look.

Honghui didn't say anything, though he did sit up. Swinging his legs over the side of the sleeping platform, he inched closer. Mulan instinctively backed up. What was he doing? Why was he getting closer? Was he . . . could he be? He came closer still. He breathed in, and for a moment, Mulan was convinced he was going to kiss her.

And then he recoiled. "You should really consider skipping guard duty and take a shower," he said. "You stink, man." Then, standing up, he slapped her on the shoulder and left.

Mulan groaned. That had taken a turn toward the mortifying. Lifting her arm, she took a quick whiff. Then she let out a louder groan. Honghui was right. She did smell. She smelled exactly like a man.

⊶◐⊕◑⊷

Something had shifted. It had started in the dining area and had continued to grow as they spoke in the sleeping tent. A friendship had begun to form between Mulan and Honghui. A friendship laced with something else Mulan wasn't sure she could name, but it was undeniable. She no longer feared Honghui, and time spent in the dining area and the sleeping barracks was easier knowing she had an ally.

On the training ground, the relationship took a different shape. It was becoming clear, to the sergeants and the soldiers, that of all the conscripts, Honghui and Mulan showed the most potential. No one was surprised by Honghui. He was built to be a warrior. Strong, intense, and with brains to match. But Mulan *was* a surprise. She was never the first or the fastest, but she always accomplished her tasks, and she did so with a quiet dignity that made others stop and take notice. As the days passed, she grew stronger, too.

Standing in the middle of the parade grounds one morning, Mulan held a spear out in front of her. The conscripts had graduated from their earlier training, when their weapons had been sticks, and were now being paired up to practice one-on-one combat with the real thing. Instinctively, Mulan and Honghui gravitated toward each other. When Sergeant Qiang gave the nod, they lifted their spears.

And then they began to fight.

Attack. Block. Attack. Block. Each move Honghui made, Mulan anticipated, lifting her own spear in a steady, smooth rhythm that Honghui met. The tempo built as they moved faster and faster. Mulan spun out of reach as Honghui kicked. Honghui blocked as Mulan came at him with her own attack. Back and forth it went, their movements oddly beautiful. They met each other with equal intensity, their eyes locked.

Unaware that others had stopped their own fights to watch, Mulan and Honghui continued to go at each other. Harder, faster, fiercer they fought, each determined to make the other one falter. Soldiers cheered on the pair. Hearing the commotion, Commander Tung emerged from his tent and came to stand beside Sergeant Qiang. They exchanged looks before the commander focused on Mulan. Sweat dripped down Mulan's brow, and he could see her shoulders shaking, but the concentration on her face didn't falter.

Mulan swung, catching Honghui off guard. He

stumbled back and for a moment, it seemed Mulan had the advantage. But in one smooth move, he swung back around and knocked her spear to the ground.

Throwing his hands in the air and letting out a shout of victory, Honghui didn't see Mulan reach down and grab the spear again. Nor did he see the determination on her face and the renewed focus. But Commander Tung did. He saw the look and quietly cheered her on.

With a shout, Mulan went after Honghui. Her ferocity was unparalleled, and Honghui had no choice but to go on the defensive, lifting his weapon to block as Mulan spun her spear through the air. Letting out a shout, she ran at him and jumped. . . .

For a moment, she appeared to hang in the air, as if held aloft by wings. And then, in a move so fast it was nothing but a blur, she brought her spear whipping down. There was a loud crack as spear met spear, and then a gasp as Honghui's weapon was sent flying from his hand. It twirled across the parade ground, end over end. As the men cheered, Mulan leapt again, only this time she, too, spun in the air, her foot coming out and meeting the still flying spear. Whipping her foot fast and furiously, she kicked the blunt end of the spear, sending it hurtling through the air with speed and power. It slammed into the side of a pole with a ping and stayed there, embedded deep in the wood.

Mulan landed on the ground. As she did so, she slammed her spear into the earth. The men's cheers stopped. They stood openmouthed as they looked from Mulan to Honghui and back again.

Catching her breath, Mulan felt the adrenaline leave her body. Slowly, she became aware of the soldiers' eyes on her. She cringed. She had let her need to win and her confusing feelings for Honghui overpower her. She had gotten carried away and brought unwanted attention to herself. That was the *last* thing she needed—especially now, when she was just beginning to feel like she could fit in.

Mumbling an apology in Honghui's general direction, Mulan ducked her head and hurried away. Behind her, the rest of the men watched, shocked into silence. What, they all wondered, had they just witnessed?

THIRTEEN

Every time Mulan closed her eyes, she saw herself spinning through the air and felt the ground crunch under her feet as she slammed down. She saw the varied looks of the other soldiers—some surprised, some awed, some bothered. But more than anything, she saw Honghui staring at her, and it was that look that lingered in her memory. He had seemed surprised. As if he hadn't thought her capable of defeating him. She didn't know whether that made her feel proud, or a bit offended. Either way, his look—and the others'—now haunted her.

She still wasn't sure what had come over her. Her body had started moving on its own. It was as though a switch had been flipped and all the training and practice had clicked into place. But there was something more to it. Something that felt deeper and bigger than her. When she had been twirling through the air, whipping her spear as though it were an extension of her body, it felt the same as the day long ago when she had chased the chicken through her family's compound and fallen off the roof. Then, like now, she had been unable to explain what had possessed her.

And that scared her.

Now she lay on her sleeping platform, willing her eyes to close. But every time she shifted, her own body odor assailed her nostrils. She needed to wash herself—and the day—off. Swinging her legs over the platform, she grabbed fresh clothes and tiptoed past the other soldiers out of the barracks.

The encampment was quiet and empty, all of the soldiers retired to their tents for the night, so Mulan was able to move quickly. Her footsteps barely made a sound as she floated over the ground toward the lake at the edge of the camp. A bright moon in the sky above illuminated its still surface. Mulan smiled at the sight of the fresh water.

Taking a quick peek over her shoulder to make sure no one was looking, Mulan undressed. Dropping her clothes in a pile, she slipped into the chilly water.

A sigh of pure bliss escaped her lips. The water washed away the dirt that clung to her skin, and the chill felt good on her aching muscles. Sinking beneath the surface, she let the silence envelope her. She floated there, suspended between the murky lake bottom and the surface above for a long moment, her thoughts slowing. There, in the silence, she was once again just Mulan. Not Hua Jun trying to prove "himself." She hadn't realized how hard the act had been on her mentally until now, when she allowed her body and mind to relax.

When her breath ran out, she allowed her body to rise and returned to the lake's surface. Keeping her eyes closed, she felt the air dry the water on her cheeks. Her hair, heavy from the liquid, made her scalp hurt and she reached for her topknot, eager to let it loose. But just as her fingers touched the long black strands, she heard a voice call out over the water.

"Hua Jun!"

Mulan's eyes snapped open. Scanning the shoreline, she spotted Honghui. "We need to talk!" he shouted as he took off his own clothes.

Panic filled Mulan. Immediately, she tried to submerge her body while simultaneously averting her eyes from Honghui. He shed his clothes quickly and with no shame.

"I came here to be alone—" Mulan called out, splashing water as she tried to move away. Desperately, she looked around for something, anything, to cover her body.

Honghui ignored her protest. Jumping into the water, he swam toward her. "What *was* that today?" he said as his arms sliced through the water. "You were incredible."

"I don't want to talk about it," Mulan said, turning so her back was to him.

Stopping a few feet away, Honghui treaded water. He looked at her with curiosity. When Mulan didn't make a move to turn toward him, Honghui swam around to face her. But she mirrored his movements, keeping her back to him. He pressed on anyway. "Teach me how you did it. Show me."

Mulan shook her head. "Leave me alone," she repeated. The words came out harsher than she had intended. But Honghui was not bothered.

"Why?" he asked. "What's wrong with you? I thought we were friends."

"I'm not your friend!" Mulan shouted. Her voice echoed over the water, bouncing back to her. She cringed. She knew as well as Honghui that that wasn't true. They *were* friends. Or at least, they were becoming friends. She peeked over her shoulder and saw confusion in Honghui's eyes. She knew it hurt, but she was trying to protect him. He couldn't find out her secret. It would mean disgrace for them both.

As Mulan remained silent and the air grew tense, Honghui's confusion turned to anger. "Then look me in the eye and say that," he demanded. Mulan did not speak. "I'm not leaving here until you look me in the eye and tell me we're not friends."

Mulan swallowed. She knew Honghui meant it. He would stay there for as long as it took to get her to turn to him.

But what could she do? Then Mulan saw a

flash of white moving along the surface of the water. Lifting her eyes, she saw the Phoenix. The bird folded its wings and dove toward the water's surface. She pierced the water behind Honghui with a *SPLASH!*

Hearing the sound, Honghui spun around. He peered into the water, trying to see beneath the surface. But the Phoenix's plunge had stirred the lake bottom and turned the water murky. "What was that?" Honghui asked, nervously scanning the water's surface. "There's something down there!" Then his eyes grew wide and he let out a shout as the Phoenix nibbled at his legs. Not waiting to see what was biting him, Honghui turned and began to swim frantically to the shore. When he reached dry land, he grabbed his clothes and raced away, not even daring a glance back.

Watching him go, Mulan breathed a sigh of relief. That had been close. She shuddered to think what would have happened if not for the Phoenix. As if on cue, the bird surfaced in front of her.

Preening herself, the Phoenix shot Mulan a satisfied smirk, as if to say, *There are worse ways a bird could spend its time*. Mulan laughed. "Thank you," she said, her tone genuine. The bird lifted into the air and, with one last conspiratorial wink, flew off, following Honghui back toward the camp.

Mulan sighed. The Phoenix had helped her out of that jam. But what was she going to do when she saw Honghui in the morning? He would be hurt, and his resentment would turn to anger. She had only *just* begun to find her place in the camp. And then she had gone and done that ridiculous thing with the spear . . . and now this? She just couldn't get out of her own way. She sighed again. She really had messed things up—and now she was going to have to pay the price.

It felt as though Mulan had only just closed her eyes when she heard the shout to wake up. Biting back a groan, she pulled herself up. Around her, the other soldiers were throwing on their clothes and armor, lacing up boots and grabbing their various equipment. Spotting Honghui, Mulan ducked her head, trying to avoid eye contact.

But the space was small, and it was impossible for them to avoid each other completely. Heading for the row of boots, Mulan leaned down and almost gasped when her shoulder accidentally brushed Honghui's. She jumped back and was about to retreat to her sleeping platform when Sergeant Qiang's voice boomed through the barracks.

"Hua Jun!" he shouted. Mulan snapped to attention and looked over. "Report to Commander Tung."

Mulan walked out of the tent, but not before catching Honghui's eye. She wasn't sure, but she almost thought she saw a flicker of compassion cross his face. But as quickly as it appeared, the flicker faded, replaced with coldness. Her shoulders sagged. What had she expected? For Honghui to suddenly forgive her for acting cold last night, just because she was now possibly walking to her doom?

Keeping her head down, she made her way across the campground toward Commander Tung's tent. While his rank afforded him lavish sleeping quarters, the commander had kept his space simple and modest. As she entered, Mulan noticed that the furnishings were bare, and it appeared as if the sleeping platform had never been used. Commander Tung was a soldier. Sleep would wait until after the battle had been won.

Sitting at his desk, the commander looked up as he heard Mulan approach. He gestured for her to come closer. Then, setting his writing utensil down, he put his hands flat on the desk. Mulan resisted the urge to run.

Finally, he spoke. "I've watched you, Hua Jun," he began. "You train hard—your spirit is evident." He paused, as though weighing his next words and their impact. "But something holds you back. It seems . . . you've been hiding something."

Mulan felt her mouth opening and closing like a fish on dry land. What did he mean? What did he *know*? She stood there, unsure what to do. She feared that at any moment, soldiers would burst into the tent to drag her away in disgrace. "Commander . . ." she started to say.

Unaware of the impact his words had had on her, the commander held up a hand for silence. "I sensed it the moment I met you. But now I am sure," Commander Tung continued. "You see, I have a secret as well. . . ." The commander looked directly into Mulan's eyes. "I know your father." At Mulan's surprised expression, Commander Tung nodded. "Hua Zhou and I fought together. He was a great soldier. In you, Hua Jun, I see the shadow of his sword. Perhaps this shadow falls heavy on your shoulders."

Bowing her head, Mulan dared not meet the commander's gaze. She didn't want him to see the emotion that filled her face. He had no idea how true his words were, though they were not true for the reason he thought. Her father's love, not his shadow, fell heavy on her. As did the truth she could not share.

Taking her silence for agreement, Commander Tung went on. "You can't allow your father's legacy to hold you back. You need to cultivate your gift."

Gift? Mulan looked up, confusion replacing her sadness. "Sir?" she asked.

"Your *chi*, Hua Jun," Commander Tung answered. "It's powerful. Why do you hide it?"

Once again, Mulan felt herself at a loss for words. Chi. The vital life force believed to flow through everyone. She had heard her father speak of warriors who possessed a stronger force than others. Warriors whose chi allowed them to be faster and braver in battle and to move with such grace and power that they could, at times, appear to hang in the air as though flying. For the commander to imply that she had such chi seemed . . . impossible. But as she stood there, the smallest of flames began to flicker. It *would* explain so much. The Phoenix. Her battle with Honghui. Maybe, just maybe, Commander Tung wasn't wrong. But she couldn't risk revealing anything special about her, or she risked revealing everything.

"I . . . I don't know," she said.

Sensing her struggle, Commander Tung nodded in understanding. "We will expose it. Allow it to blossom. The truth never hurts as much as the exposure of a lie." With a nod, he dismissed Mulan.

Slowly she left, the commander's words ringing in her head. He had not guessed her secret, but for some reason, she felt as if he had revealed something far deeper.

FOURTEEN

"The chi pervades the universe and all living things."

The morning after their conversation, Commander Tung called the conscripts out to the parade grounds. Arranging them in a circle around him, he moved in a series of slow, intricate motions. As he moved, he spoke. The conscripts watched, mesmerized by the way the commander's body seemed to be one with his weapon. His sword became an extension of his arm; his legs, like roots of a tree, were firmly planted on the ground until they lifted and appeared to become light as feathers. He signaled to them, and Mulan and the others began to mirror his moves.

"We are all born with it," Commander Tung continued. "But only the most dedicated will connect deeply to his chi and become a great warrior."

Mulan focused, her body moving of its own accord. She heard the commander's voice roll over her like the water of the lake, with the same soothing effect. "Tranquil as a forest," he said. "But on fire within."

Swinging her arm though the air, Mulan practiced the simple movements over and over again. She trained through the afternoon and then later, as she stood guard. When her shift was over, she made her way back to the lake, where she practiced under the light of the moon. With every swish of her sword, she felt her chi grow stronger. It blossomed, like the leaves on the magnolia tree by the lake's shore. The sensation was empowering and strange, like something wholly new but also oddly familiar.

Over the days that followed, the conscripts' training intensified. It was a subtle shift at first. A few more minutes tacked onto the end of each session. A bit more bark—and bite—from Sergeant Qiang as he shouted orders. Tensions rose as it became clear that they were no longer practicing for a possible battle but for an actual one.

"The Rouran enemy is vast," Sergeant Qiang warned as Mulan and the others went through a series of martial arts movements. "They're ruthless and unpredictable. Yet physical force need not be met with equal force. The warrior yields to force—and redirects it." He stopped in front of Mulan. She kept her gaze ahead, not allowing him to intimidate her.

Ever since she and Commander Tung had spoken, Mulan had been able to think of nothing but her chi. It consumed her. Fueled her. Drove her. Every moment she could spare, she spent trying to focus it. The commander's words had been like a spark. She'd realized, in the moments after they talked, that she owed it to her father to be the best warrior she could be. If she didn't try for that, then everything she had done would be in vain. So, night after night, day after day, she practiced. And night after night, day after day, she grew stronger.

Under the moonlight, beside the lake, she moved her body through maneuvers that now felt natural. In her head, she heard Sergeant Qiang's words. *Disadvantage can be turned to advantage,* he would tell the soldiers as they pressed their swords forward, swished their spears through the air, lifted their shields in defense.

Her constant practice and intense focus did not go unnoticed. She felt Commander Tung's and Sergeant Qiang's eyes on her more than on the others. But it no longer made her shrink inward. She felt fueled with courage and a strength she hadn't known she had.

But there was still one challenge that stymied her.

"Four ounces can move a thousand pounds," the sergeant said as Mulan and the others approached the steep steps that led to the shrine. They all paused, their eyes lifting in unison to the challenge in front of them. On either side of Mulan was a bucket filled to the brim with water. Above her, other soldiers grabbed their own buckets and struggled up the steps. Mulan waited. Sergeant

Qiang's words echoed in her head. "Four ounces can move a thousand pounds," she whispered to herself. Closing her eyes, she focused. She felt the now familiar surge of energy wash through her as she connected to her chi. The grunts and groans from the other men vanished. She felt only the gentle breeze on her cheeks. Her eyes still closed, she envisioned the top of the shrine. She remembered the peace she'd felt beneath the magnolia tree. Channeling that, she opened her eyes.

Bending down, she grasped the handles of the buckets and lifted them. They felt lighter than they had the first few times she had faced this challenge, thanks to her strength training. But she knew that the challenge was not in the first steps, but in the endurance one must have to make it all the way to the top. Step by step, she climbed.

Ahead of her, the other conscripts' steps slowed. One by one, they began to fall. First Cricket, his face wet with tears, sank to the steps. Then Po, who threw his buckets aside and simply lay down, defeated. Yao was the next to fail. Filled with rage, he threw his buckets, the wood shattering against the rocky cliffs.

Still, Mulan continued. Her steps were steady, her shoulders still. On either side of her the water in the buckets did not splash over the sides, but instead remained calm. She grew stronger with each step. The focus on her face never faltered, even as she moved past her fallen comrades.

Soon the only other conscript left was Honghui. A few steps ahead of her, his forehead was beaded with sweat and his buckets were sinking closer and closer to the ground. His steps were heavy and his breathing ragged. Like Mulan, his face was focused, but doubt was beginning to creep in.

Mulan didn't notice any of that. She kept moving. Step by step, higher and higher, gathering strength until she caught up to Honghui—and then passed him. She felt his gaze on her back as she continued. She ignored it. She was somewhere else. Her body was on the stairs, her arms holding the buckets, but her mind was in a deeper place. She was fueled by thoughts of her father, her mother, her sister. Even thoughts of the Phoenix, who was inextricably connected to her and who had found a strength of her own.

Behind her, Honghui's body gave out. He sank to the steps. Now, it was only Mulan left. As

Honghui, Commander Tung, Sergeant Qiang, and all the others watched, Mulan kept climbing. Step by step, higher and higher, until . . .

She reached the top.

For a long moment, Mulan stood, her chest rising and falling evenly. She turned around, her eyes growing wide as she took in the breathtaking view from the top of the shrine. Her eyes paused as she spotted the Phoenix perched on a nearby statue. Spreading her feathers wide, the Phoenix called out in triumph.

Pride flooded through Mulan. She had done it. She had done what no man had been able to. She, Mulan, a girl from a small village, had made the impossible possible. She turned back to look at the soldiers gathered below. Only then, as she saw the looks of wonder, awe, and amazement on their faces, did she allow herself a smile.

Commander Tung's thoughts swirled in his head. Hua Jun had done it. He had conquered the shrine. In all his years training soldiers, he had only seen a handful of men accomplish the task. And none of them had done so with the grace and focus Hua

Jun had demonstrated. Turning away from the shrine, the commander walked toward his tent. Sergeant Qiang fell into step beside him.

"Hua Jun is a true leader," the sergeant observed. He, too, had been impressed by the soldier's success.

Commander Tung nodded. "Yes. He has the same spirit as his father—a warrior." He paused, his face thoughtful. "But I sense something still holds him back."

"Perhaps in time he'll overcome the obstacle," Sergeant Qiang said after a moment.

The commander's steps stopped, and he turned to look at his second-in-command. "We're out of time," he said. "The enemy advances. We deploy at first light."

He didn't need to say more. With a nod, Sergeant Qiang turned and ordered the soldiers to the parade grounds. Despite their exhaustion, the men jumped to attention and made their way over as fast as their tired legs could take them. Mulan arrived last, having had to climb down from the shrine.

When all the conscripts were gathered, Commander Tung took his place in front of them.

"Our training is not finished," he said. "But we live during a time of war. Therefore, we shift with changing winds." He paused to make sure he had everyone's attention. Satisfied the men were listening, he went on. "We leave to defend the Mountain Steppe Garrison."

The response was swift. Surprise, fear, and excitement spread through the men. Whispers and murmurs rose over them like a wave. This was what they had been waiting for—and dreading. From her spot at the back of the crowd, Mulan felt her cheeks grow pale. The energy and strength she had only just been feeling faded. It was one thing to accomplish a training task. It was an entirely different thing to face actual battle.

Commander Tung lifted a hand. The men grew silent once more. "You will now take the Oath of the Warrior, pledging fidelity to the Three Pillars of Virtue." The commander pulled out his sword. Mulan's eyes widened as she realized it was identical to her father's. Sensing her eyes on him, Commander Tung looked over and nodded ever so subtly in her direction. "Without each one of these pillars, your vital chi is diminished."

One by one, the student warriors unsheathed

their swords and held them high. As Mulan lifted her own, she saw the inscription glittering in the sun. Her eyes read the words as, in front of them, Tung said them aloud. "Brave!" he shouted.

The soldiers, including Mulan, echoed the word back to him.

"Loyal!" Again, after the commander's shout, the soldiers shouted back.

A sense of dread began to build in Mulan's stomach as she saw the word that would be shouted next. "True!" Commander Tung finished.

Around her, all the other soldiers yelled out the word, their voices full of emotion and pride. But Mulan stayed quiet. How could she swear to be true when she was living a lie?

FIFTEEN

Mulan's thoughts were still twirling the next morning as they marched out of the camp and toward the Mountain Steppe Garrison. The footsteps of the newly made soldiers provided background noise to her pounding heart.

Her deceit was weighing her down more than the bag on her back. She wanted to stay quiet, but she felt as though she should come clean. These men had become her friends. Commander Tung and Sergeant Qiang had become mentors. She was betraying them all, and to give her full attention on the battlefield, she needed a clear mind. Yet, silence was her friend, too. Not speaking would allow her to keep her secret, while the other choice would result in a punishment worse than death . . . disgrace.

She looked ahead to where Honghui marched, his head up, his eyes clear. What, she wondered, would *he* do? What advice would he give her if she were to ask? Then an image of the Phoenix flashed in her mind. Would her ancestors want her to reveal who she was? Or would they want her to live a lie? By the time they stopped to make camp for the night, Mulan had made her decision.

Walking over to the commander's tent, she paused. Taking a deep breath, she composed herself. "Commander Tung," she said, announcing herself. "It's Hua Jun."

"You may enter, Hua Jun." Commander Tung's response was quick and curt.

Entering the tent, Mulan nodded at her commanding officer. His attention was focused on his sword, which lay across his lap. He was sharpening it with smooth, methodical strokes.

"Commander Tung," Mulan began. "There is something that weighs heavily on my heart. I need to confess it to you." Her mouth grew dry as the commander looked up at her. She opened and closed her mouth several times, trying desperately to make her tongue form the right words. "It has to do with the Three Virtues. . . ." That was as far as she could get.

As she struggled, Commander Tung watched. To her surprise, she saw compassion in his eyes, as if seeing her struggle hurt him. Getting to his feet, the commander approached her. "There's no shame in being fearful before battle," he said, mistaking the reason for her visit. "In fact, it's a testament to your honesty that you confess such doubt."

His words stabbed at Mulan's already guilty conscience. Honesty? She was there to tell him how *dishonest* she was. She shook her head, trying to get the conversation back on track and say what she needed to say. "Yes, Commander," she said, "but the other virtues—"

Commander Tung interrupted her. "Hua Jun," he said, his tone serious. "I've been doing this a long time. I stake my career on my ability to judge character. You're a good man. Perhaps one day you'll accompany me to my village, where I will introduce you to my daughter."

His daughter? Mulan's jaw dropped. Those were the last words she had anticipated coming out of his mouth.

"And our village matchmaker, of course," Commander Tung finished.

Mulan's knees buckled as she understood what the commander's words implied. Not knowing how to respond, she bowed. She had no choice but to nod her head. "It would be my great honor, Commander."

He smiled, relief on his face. Mulan realized that he had been oddly nervous to say such a thing to her. It made the lie she was living feel still more shameful. She had come to tell him the truth, and yet somehow ended up further into the mess her lie had created.

"I'll look forward to the look on your father's face when you give him this news," the commander said, bringing the conversation to a close.

Slipping outside the tent, Mulan let out a shaky breath. As she did, she saw the Phoenix standing a few feet away. The bird had overheard the entire exchange. She gave Mulan a look that clearly said, *Really?*

"Well, what was I supposed to do?" Mulan whispered.

The Phoenix shot her another look. This one was even easier to read. *I don't know. Maybe not agree to get married to a woman.*

"Thank you for your support," Mulan said, this time not bothering to whisper or keep the sarcasm from her voice. "Really."

But the Phoenix was right. She shouldn't have said yes. She should have told the truth like she had planned to. Instead, she had let the lie live, and now things couldn't possibly get worse.

◦┉◉┉✦┉◉┉◦

Fortunately, Mulan wasn't given time to dwell on the growing chaos of her situation. Arriving back at her tent, she had only a few hours of restless sleep before the soldiers were once again awoken and ordered to move out.

They marched through the desert steppe, the dry, shrub-covered ground offering them little protection from the elements, or any potential enemy eyes. Mulan's gaze drifted over the arid landscape as they walked, her mind feeling as drained as the land around her. After a few hours' march, the land began to rise beneath their feet, the shrubs giving way to a rocky landscape. In the distance, the Mountain Steppe Garrison rose up, protected on one side by mountains but left vulnerable in the front.

Arriving in front of the garrison entrance, Commander Tung lifted a hand. Mulan and the others came to a halt as they waited for the soldiers to open the heavy gates. As the wooden doors opened, the inside of the garrison came into view. It was like any other garrison under the Emperor's rule. Filled with vendors selling their goods and a few smaller buildings, it was busy, but not bustling. In one corner, Mulan spotted a tavern. Then her eyes grew wide and she let out a happy shout.

"Black Wind!"

As the other soldiers looked around for what had caused her outburst, Mulan raced across the garrison toward the tavern. Her horse stood tied up in front. Hearing her voice, he let out a happy nicker and pulled back against the reins, trying to free himself. Mulan threw her arms around him, breathing in his familiar and comforting scent. Finally, she pulled away. Her hand still gently rubbing the horse's neck, her eyes shifted toward the tavern door. Then they narrowed. She knew exactly who was inside.

Giving Black Wind one last pat and promising she would be back, Mulan stormed inside the tavern. She spotted Skatch and Ramtish immediately. They were sitting at a table, staring down at a map. Their robes and beards seemed dirtier than when she had last seen them. Mulan approached, her steps determined. Ramtish spotted her, and her expression grew more furious as she saw him shift uncomfortably in his seat.

"Remember that conscript, that kid . . ." she heard Ramtish say to Skatch.

The other man nodded. "Hua Jun," he said.

"Remember you taught him to stand his ground, own the place?" he said. Skatch mumbled a yes but kept staring at the map. Ramtish went on. "Tip of the blade and all that?"

"So?" Skatch said, sounding annoyed to be distracted.

"He took it to heart," Ramtish finished.

Skatch looked up—right into the glaring eyes

of Mulan. "Hua Jun!" he said, jumping to his feet, a nervous smile on his face.

Mulan didn't return the smile. As Honghui, Yao, Po, Ling, and Cricket entered behind her, Mulan leapt into the air and in one swift move, kicked Skatch with both her feet. Hard. He fell back, landing on the floor with a thud. His fake beard, knocked loose by the impact, hung from his chin. Turning, Mulan set her sights on Ramtish. The man instantly held up his hands.

"Not the face—" he started to say.

But Mulan didn't let him finish. She leapt again and, this time, spun in the air before kicking Ramtish in the chest. His own fake beard went flying, landing in the middle of a table of very confused onlookers.

As the pair of thieves stared at her with a mixture of awe and fear, Mulan turned and walked out of the tavern. Behind her she could hear the other soldiers picking up Skatch and Ramtish. By the time she had found Commander Tung, the two fake monks had been put in stock collars, their heads hanging uncomfortably between the wooden planks.

"Tell us what happened, Hua Jun," Commander

Tung said as the sun set over the garrison courtyard. Beside him stood the garrison commander. Sergeant Qiang and the other soldiers were a few paces away, watching with curiosity.

Mulan stepped forward. "I met these two bandits on the road," she explained, shooting them a look. "They offered me food and drink, and . . ." She paused, her voice unsure. She didn't want to admit they had fooled her into believing they were monks, and worse, tricked her into drinking. That would make her look weak and ridiculous. "And . . ." she stammered.

To her surprise, Skatch jumped in. "Hua Jun showed us a rare generosity of spirit," he said, looking up at her through the hair that fell over his eyes. "Offering a place by his fire. In return, we betrayed his trust."

Mulan's eyes widened. Skatch was protecting her honor. But why? What good did that do him? She looked over at him, curious to see what he would say next.

"It is true," Skatch went on. "We are not monks. We are, in fact, bandits. An odd career choice, perhaps, but it's a time-honored profession. We bandits are an integral element of the Silk Road. Eliminate us, and the delicate fabric of the entire enterprise unravels."

Unbelievable, Mulan thought. Somehow, Skatch was making it sound like his job of stealing was an honorable one. A task that others *needed* him to perform. She looked at Commander Tung's face and saw that he, too, looked incredulous.

Ramtish, whose face wore an expression Mulan couldn't quite make out, nodded. "Might I add, Commander, that we could also have taken the lad's sword, but I—personally—felt that would be wrong."

Mulan resisted the urge to laugh out loud. She very much doubted that was the case. True, she didn't know these men well, but she would have put money on Skatch being the one who had left her the sword. Of the two, he had seemed the more gentlemanly, if that term could even be used for such heathens.

Noticing that the commander and the others were losing patience, Skatch went on, pleading his case. "Accordingly, if Hua Jun finds it in his heart to forgive us"—he paused and turned to Commander

Tung—"and the wise commander sees his way clear to pardoning us, we can proceed with removing these restraints. . . ."

The commander had heard enough. He raised a hand, silencing Skatch. Looking at Sergeant Qiang, he called him over. "Sergeant, what is the penalty for stealing a soldier's horse during wartime?" he asked.

"Death," Sergeant Qiang replied.

In the stocks, Skatch's and Ramtish's now beardless faces grew pale. Mulan's eyes widened.

"Hua Jun," Commander Tung said, turning to her. "Did these miscreants steal your horse?"

Mulan hesitated, but after a second, she nodded. "Yes," she said.

She was kept from saying more by the sudden shout of a soldier behind her. "Scouts at the gate!" A moment later, the large doors swung open and two men raced through. Their horses were lathered in sweat, their own faces ashen. Dismounting, they raced over to the commander.

"Böri Khan assembles not a half day's ride from here," the first scout reported. "They prepare for battle. We are greatly outnumbered."

Instantly, the soldiers began to murmur.

Turning to the guards stationed at the top of the gate, the garrison commander shouted, "Fortify for a siege!" His voice was filled with fear, causing the men around him to grow nervous.

Beside him, Commander Tung remained calm. Once again, he lifted his hand. Instantly, the garrison grew quiet. "No!" he said to the garrison commander. "We will appear where we are unexpected. Let Khan charge our wall of spears on ground of our choosing. He who moves first controls the enemy." He paused and looked out over his soldiers, his gaze lingering longest on Mulan. Then he turned back to Sergeant Qiang. "Prepare the men," he ordered.

The soldiers didn't hesitate. Instantly, they moved into action, readying for battle. But the sergeant hesitated. Mulan saw him nod toward Skatch and Ramtish, who stood forgotten in the stocks. "Commander Tung—the bandits?" he asked.

The commander barely registered the question, distracted by the news. But Mulan did. And she saw a way to perhaps save the two men from the penalty of death. She didn't like them, but she didn't want their deaths on her conscience. Stepping forward, she addressed Commander Tung. "If I may, Commander . . ." she began. He nodded for her to go on. "Since we are greatly outnumbered, perhaps these able-bodied miscreants can be of help?"

A look of surprise and approval crossed over Commander Tung's face. He nodded. "Good thinking. If they perish on the battlefield, at least they'll have been of some service. Arm them." His order given, the commander moved off. Behind him, a pair of soldiers removed the stocks from Skatch and Ramtish. Both looked upset by their sudden freedom.

"Arm them?" Skatch said, repeating Commander Tung's words.

"As in, 'fight the Rourans'?" Ramtish added. He shook his head, trying desperately to get back *in* the stocks.

Beside him, Skatch did the same. "Might I suggest all options be considered before we embark on such a hasty decision?" he said to the soldiers.

"Surely there are other ways we can be of service," Ramtish added. "In fact, we could . . ." He struggled to think of something, anything else they could do to help. "Clean up the horse poop!"

"Yes!" Skatch said, jumping on the idea. "The overabundance of manure on the battlefield is an issue that's been pushed into the shadows for far too long—"

Mulan couldn't take any more. "Enough!" she said. To her surprise, both men quieted. "You protected me. Now I have protected you." She pulled out her sword. "Don't make me regret it." Turning, she went to join the others.

As she walked away, she could feel Skatch's approving eyes on her. She bit back a smile. They were obnoxious, but they were not horrible people. They didn't deserve to die in the stocks. She had saved them from that. Now they would just have to use their conniving ways to make sure they didn't perish on the battlefield.

SIXTEEN

In the Rouran camp, warriors also readied for battle. Swords were being sharpened and bows were being stretched. Böri Khan was also preparing. He stood with his bare chest glistening as he washed himself. It was a ritual, one that allowed him to brace himself both physically and mentally for the fight ahead.

Khan was pleased. His army had grown, and now hundreds of yurts filled with hundreds of men dotted the harsh landscape around him. It had taken him more time than he had hoped, but with the death of Duba Tegin he had ensured the loyalty of all the tribes.

Now they just needed to take over the Empire.

Hearing the familiar screech of a hawk, he turned as the bird flew into his tent. As he watched, the creature transformed. Wings became arms, claws turned to feet, and soon Xianniang stood in front of him.

"You have news from the garrison?" Khan asked, not stopping his washing.

The witch nodded. She had been on patrol for most of the night and looked bothered to not have his complete attention. "New soldiers," she reported. "Children. It will fall. Before the new moon you will take the kingdom. You will have your revenge. If our plan continues."

At her words, Böri Khan's hand stilled and he lifted his gaze to meet hers. He didn't like the defiant edge to her tone. "What threatens our plan?" he asked. As he spoke, he took a menacing step toward the witch.

"I must be able to trust you," Xianniang said,

her tone cold. She did not shrink away from Böri Khan's hulking body, but she did lift her chest higher, as though trying to match him.

"You *can't* trust me," he replied, taking some small satisfaction from the surprise that flickered over the witch's face. "But you have no choice. When I found you out on the desert steppe, wandering alone, you were exiled. A scorned dog. Your powers meant *nothing* without me." He stopped, his words hanging heavy in the air. He stared down at Xianniang, waiting for her response.

In a flash, Xianniang's talons were out and wrapped around his neck. "I could tear you to pieces before you blink," she hissed.

Böri Khan felt the talons at his throat and saw the anger in the witch's eyes. But he remained calm. When he spoke, his voice was even—and ice cold. "Remember what you want. A place where your powers will not be vilified. A place where you are accepted for who you are." He watched the witch's expression grow angrier as the words she had said to him in confidence echoed back at her. "You won't get what you want without me. And do you want to know why?" He paused, though he knew she wouldn't answer. "No army will follow a *woman.*" He let his words hang in the air. "Trust me or not, I'm your only option."

Böri Khan watched as the anger dimmed in her eyes. Xianniang knew he was right.

"Remember you also need me, Böri Khan," she replied after a short pause, her grip still tight on his neck.

"I don't deny it," Böri Khan said.

They held each other's gaze for a moment longer. Xianniang withdrew her talons from Böri Khan's throat.

"We will finish what we started," she said.

This time, Böri Khan gave a nod. "Yes," he agreed. "And you will see to it that nothing—and no one—stands in our way."

Pushing past her, Böri Khan put on a tunic and strode over to the door of the yurt. Yes, things were falling into place. He had his army. He had his witch. And soon he would have his kingdom.

Mulan stared out at the thick mist in front of her. The sun tried to cut through the gray, making it hard to see what was shadow and what was real. Astride Black Wind, Mulan could make out a bit more than the soldiers on the ground could. But not much more.

She had been surprised when Commander Tung had ordered them to stop in the middle of the mist-filled valley. It seemed like that would put them at a disadvantage strategically. But apparently not. This way, the commander told them, the element of surprise would be on their side. They knew which direction the Rouran army was coming from, whereas the enemy had no idea what now lay in wait.

As the sun grew stronger, it burned off the mist. Slowly, the shadows disappeared. Mulan's breath caught in her throat as the last of the wisps disappeared, revealing a massive army across from the Imperial battalion. The Rourans seemed to cover the entire horizon, banners of dozens of tribes whipping in the air.

In front of them all was Böri Khan. He sat astride his midnight-black stallion, his eyes cold and calculating, even from such a distance. Mulan tensed, and beneath her, Black Wind shifted nervously on his feet. As part of the cavalry, Mulan would be in one of the last groups to charge. But it didn't matter when in the order she would go.

Now that she had seen the enemy, the last tiny sliver of hope that she might avoid battle had faded.

Turning, she saw her friends standing among the infantry: Po, Yao, and Ling. The usual confidence was gone from their faces, replaced with apprehension. Scanning further still, Mulan saw Skatch and Ramtish. Without their fake beards or monk robes, they seemed smaller somehow. And fear was etched in every weather-worn line on their faces. Mulan felt a flash of sympathy for the pair. They had wanted no part of this war, and yet she had brought it to them. If they survived the battle to come, she vowed, she would figure out a way to apologize—even if she still hadn't forgiven them for stealing Black Wind.

Her eyes stopped on Honghui. To her surprise, he was staring back at her. For a moment, they held each other's gaze. The other sounds faded away, and all Mulan could hear were the uneven gasps of her own breath and the pounding of her heart. She saw in Honghui's eyes the same questioning look, the same unspoken apology, that she knew hers held. Both recognized this might very well be the last time they ever saw each other alive. And in that moment of realization, all the competition and animosity fell away. In its place was something neither would have dared give voice to: respect . . . but also something deeper. Something they couldn't explain, but that caused Mulan to feel flushed and made Honghui shift on his feet.

The sound of drums boomed through the valley, startling Mulan. She dropped her gaze from Honghui's. Pushing aside the strange sensation settling in her stomach, Mulan turned back to the valley and the enemy beyond. It was time to focus.

The battle was here.

As the drumming grew louder and faster, the front line of Imperial soldiers kneeled. Behind them, the archers stepped forward, readying their bows. Cricket stood in the middle of them, his eyes clear, his shoulders steady. Mulan couldn't help being impressed. The boy had become a warrior.

Commander Tung raised his hand. The army seemed to take a collective breath. And then, the commander gave the signal. As the Imperial flag waved down, the archers let their arrows fly. They arched high over the valley—now a battlefield— toward the Rouran army beyond.

If Commander Tung thought this first wave

of attack would intimidate Böri Khan, he was quickly proven wrong. The Rouran warrior didn't even wait for the arrows to land before he gave his own signal. In an instant, the sound of the drums was muted by the pounding hooves of hundreds of horses as Böri Khan led his army racing across the valley.

The archers kept the arrows flying. Some found their targets, knocking Rourans from their saddles, but they barely made a dent. The Rouran army was huge. It would take more than the archers to bring it down.

Waiting anxiously for Commander Tung's signal, Mulan watched as Böri Khan shouted to a few of his men and then, with a dozen or so of the warriors, peeled off from the main body of the army. The momentum carried the rest of the army forward. Acting quickly, Commander Tung shouted orders to the cavalry—including Mulan—sending them after the Rouran leader. While the rest of the infantry and archers took their chances with the oncoming horde, the cavalry exploded after Böri Khan.

Black Wind's mane whipped behind him as Mulan rode the horse across the valley. Ahead, she could see Böri Khan, and the warriors she now recognized as the fabled Shadow Warriors noticed they were being followed. With a shout, one of them spun around so that he was riding his horse backward. As the horse galloped on, unbothered, the Shadow Warrior notched two arrows, letting them fly in quick succession.

An Imperial soldier nearby shouted as he was hit and knocked from his horse. Mulan didn't have time to register fear, as a moment later, the other arrow zipped past, barely missing her. She heard a thud as another rider fell. Still, they raced on.

As the ground changed beneath them, growing rockier, Mulan notched her own arrows. She barely took notice of the steamy, mountainous environment they had entered. She had eyes only for the Rouran warriors. More enemy soldiers were spinning on their horses, firing arrows faster and faster. The Imperial soldiers began to fall with more and more frequency. Some were felled by arrows, others when their horses tripped on the rocky terrain. Steam caused by the warm air spewing from the volcanic vents rose, clouding Mulan's vision, but still she rode on as one by one the other Imperial soldiers, deciding the Rouran leader was too far gone, turned and retreated to the battlefield.

Soon Mulan was alone.

Black Wind's pace slowed. Mulan looked over her shoulder at the other soldiers who were now racing away. The thought of following them in retreat was strong. But stronger still was the sound of Commander Tung's voice in her mind as he called out the Pillars of Virtue. It was her duty as a member of the Imperial Army to be loyal and brave. She might not be able to live up to the virtue of truth, but that didn't mean she couldn't fight for the other pillars. Dragging her gaze from the sight of the fleeing Imperial Army, she spotted Böri Khan disappearing into the steam ahead.

Screwing up her courage, she urged Black Wind on and followed.

SEVENTEEN

Mulan slowed Black Wind to a trot. The steam was too dense to see through and she didn't want to risk the big horse stumbling on one of the thermal vents that dotted the landscape. For what seemed like hours, but was no more than a few minutes, horse and rider wandered, lost, inside the steam clouds.

When the clouds cleared, Mulan gasped. The barren landscape was a riot of vibrant color. Red lava poured from vents, transforming into lines of black frozen rock as the air cooled. It was as though she had ridden into a whole other world.

And Böri Khan was nowhere to be seen.

An ear-piercing shriek filled the air. Looking up, Mulan only had a moment to register the hawk diving toward her before she was knocked from Black Wind's back. She toppled to the ground. Her helmet, knocked loose by the impact, fell from her head and tumbled across the ground. The topknot, kept restrained for so long, came undone and Mulan groaned, her hair falling over her shoulders.

Scrambling to her feet, Mulan reached for her helmet. But before she could get to it, the hawk landed in front of her. Then, as Mulan watched in disbelief, the hawk transformed into a beautiful woman. The woman appeared strong—and deadly.

"You're a witch . . ." Mulan said, the words sticking in her throat.

The woman nodded. She walked closer, looking Mulan up and down, her eyes lingering on the armor and then moving to the hair that now fell over Mulan's shoulders. Something flashed across her eyes, a revelation. "You've kept your secret.

Well done. But now you are in my way. You must retreat. Go."

Mulan's eyes widened as she realized this woman could see past her disguise. Rage built inside of her at being called out by the witch. "I am Hua Jun," Mulan said. "Soldier in the Emperor's Imperial Army."

Lifting her sword, she ran at the witch. But Xianniang fended her off. With a wave of her hand, she sent Mulan flying to the ground. Mulan let out a shout and jumped back to her feet. She would not let the witch stop her. Once again, she charged at Xianniang, and once again, the witch brushed her away.

"Your deceit weakens you," Xianniang said as she wrapped her long fingers around Mulan's neck. Mulan's heart thudded in her chest. She was weak, that much was true. Still, she wouldn't let the other woman see her fear. She met the witch's eyes as the woman went on. "You would be a fool to fight me—even at your strongest."

Lifting her sword, Mulan tried to go at the witch. But in response, Xianniang wrapped her hand around the blade and lowered it. "You waste my time," the witch said, growing frustrated.

Desperately, Mulan tugged at her sword. To her surprise, the blade came back, slicing the witch's palm. As blood bloomed on her hand, Xianniang's eyes filled with anger. "Why do you not listen?" she shouted.

Mulan scrambled backward. She used all her strength to keep the sword steady in front of her. Xianniang shrugged and then, pulling a dagger from her belt, threw it at her. Mulan tried to block it, but the force of the dagger was great, and when it contacted her sword, the dagger sent the blade flying from her hand. The sword twirled through the air, end over end, before landing on the ground, where it skittered across a thin crust of cooled lava that covered a nearby lake like ice.

Panic washed over Mulan. Her father's sword! She couldn't lose it. Not caring that she had turned her back to the witch, Mulan raced onto the lava crust. Like ice, it was slipperier than it appeared, and Mulan instantly fell, the impact causing the surface to crack around her. She knew there was no way it would hold. Not for long. But she *had* to get the sword. On her hands and knees, she inched farther out onto the crust as all around her more cracks began to appear.

Behind her, Xianniang stepped onto the cracking lava, her own steps so light that they left no impression on the thin layer of ash that covered the ground. Blood dripped from the wound Mulan had inflicted, dotting the black with red.

Mulan reached her sword. With a triumphant cry, her fingers closed around the handle and she got to her feet. Turning, she saw the witch watching her. "I am Hua Jun. Soldier in the Emperor's Imp—"

Xianniang had heard enough. "I warned you, *Hua Jun*," Xianniang sneered. "You will die pretending to be something you're not." In a flash of silver, Xianniang threw another dagger. It flew through the air, striking Mulan square in the chest.

Mulan was lifted off her feet and sent flying backward. As she came down hard, the layer of crust beneath her broke open. Mulan fell through the hole—and into the lake below.

◦❯◦◉◦⬤◦◉◦◦❮◦

Mulan's chest burned as she sank deeper and deeper beneath the lake's surface. Her hand, still clutching her father's sword, was frozen and she felt powerless. All she could do was sink, weighted down by the armor she wore.

She saw a flash of color, and then something dove into the water above her. At first, Mulan feared it was the witch, coming to finish her off. But as she watched, the shadowy shape took form, revealing itself as the Phoenix. Reaching her, the bird turned and, wrapping its long tail feathers around her wrist, pulled her upward.

A moment later, Mulan burst through the surface, opening her mouth and sucking in air. She lay on the hard ground beside the lake for a long moment, her eyes closed as her heartbeat slowed. She opened her eyes.

Instantly, she wished she hadn't.

There, protruding from her chest, was the witch's dagger.

It stuck straight out, the tip of the blade disappearing into Mulan's armor. But as she stared down, expecting any moment for blood to pour from the wound, Mulan's eyes narrowed. Lifting her shaking hands, she pulled out the dagger. Ripping back her armor, Mulan saw, to her relief, it had embedded not in her skin, but in the leather binding she had wrapped around her chest.

In a whoosh, Mulan's breath rushed out of her and she shouted a cry of gratitude. To think, the thing that she had used to lie, the thing that could have been her downfall, had just saved her life.

Slowly, she got to her feet. Turning around, she saw the Phoenix sitting a few steps away. The bird's feathers were wet and she looked tired, but happy. Meeting her gaze, Mulan gave the Phoenix a grateful nod. The bird nodded. *I've got your back, always,* she seemed to say. And for the first time, Mulan realized how much she had needed the Phoenix, now and throughout the long journey.

Lifting her sword from the ground, she read the inscription, her eyes lingering on one word. "True . . ." she said aloud. True. Yes. It was the virtue she had struggled so much with, and yet the one she longed to embrace. And now she needed to be true to herself. She wasn't going to listen to the witch's words or let doubt creep in. She needed to follow her heart.

Mulan raced over and jumped onto Black Wind's back. The horse whinnied as she urged him forward. Behind her, she heard flapping wings as the Phoenix took flight. Together, they raced across the valley in the direction of the battlefield. Her armor, loosened from the fight, fell to the ground piece by piece. The wind whipped her long hair around her face. There was no hiding who she was now. But she didn't care. She was done pretending. The witch had seen her as enough of a threat to try to kill her. She *was* strong. She was no longer Hua Jun. She was Mulan. She was a woman. And she was a warrior.

As she reached the edge of the valley, she could hear the sounds of battle from below the ridge. Riding over, Mulan pulled up Black Wind. Below, the Imperial Army was trying, in vain, to keep the Rourans at bay. Soldiers stood back to back, their swords flashing in the sunlight as they struggled to fight the Rouran attackers. Arrows continued to fly through the air but they were being shot without intention as the archers simply tried to survive.

Above it all, Mulan saw the witch, once again in her hawk form. She circled above the two armies, letting out menacing shrieks that encouraged the Rourans and made the Imperial soldiers shake in fear.

Mulan didn't hesitate. Spurring Black Wind, she raced down the hill and right into the fight. As she went, she lifted her sword and swung. On either side of her, enemies fell as metal met skin. She didn't even notice the stunned looks of Commander Tung or Honghui as they caught sight of the powerful female warrior doing what none of them had been able to—win. Caught in the moment, she appeared like a mirage through the steam that rose from the valley floor. Her hair covered her face and her arm moved so fast that she appeared a blur.

As she raced on, Black Wind's nostrils flared and his hooves pounded against the ground. Together, they looked like something magical. Reaching the heart of the battle, Mulan gathered her courage and pushed herself to her feet so that she was standing tall on her horse's back. Then, with a cry, she leapt off and flew through the air. For a moment, she hung, suspended, before landing on the ground, her sword raised in front of her.

Instantly, the Rourans rushed at her. Channeling her training and focusing on her chi, Mulan lost herself in the rhythmic swing of her sword. Around her, the men she had come to know as friends fought valiantly. Honghui's sword dispatched two Rourans at once while Yao screamed and shouted, swinging his sword wildly but effectively. Even Skatch and Ramtish were giving it all they had, kicking and scratching and throwing rocks to protect themselves.

Inch by inch, the Imperial Army seemed to gain a foothold. Whether it was the appearance of the mysterious female warrior or just luck, it didn't matter. Inches were all they needed. With renewed energy, the soldiers continued to fight. Spotting the last large group of Rouran invaders, their arms heavy with sword and shield, Mulan rushed toward them.

In a group, they turned to face the approaching warrior. But Mulan didn't slow. She kept running, and just as it seemed she was going to collide headfirst with the remaining Rouran soldiers, she once again jumped into the air. Her feet light and her mind focused, she raced atop the invaders, using their helmets and their raised shields to propel herself forward. In a flash, she had crossed over all of them and leapt to the ground.

Furious, the Rourans turned and started chasing after her.

Mulan allowed herself a small smile. This was what she had wanted. Sprinting toward the other edge of the valley, she ran onto a large rock formation. On the other side was a wall of steam.

A gust of wind blew back the steam for a moment, revealing a large crack in the ground. Mulan hesitated only briefly before leaping. Behind her, the steam moved back over the ground, concealing the crack from view.

Behind her, the invaders' angry cries grew louder as they saw their prey disappear. With bloodlust in their eyes, they followed, running up and jumping off the rock. But their cries of anger turned to fear as they fell, one by one, into the deep crack just beyond the rock. The crack, formed from the pressure of the lava, billowed steam upward as it pulled the Rourans down. In seconds, the invading warriors had been lost to the earth.

On the other side, standing with her sword still raised, was Mulan, ready for the next onslaught. Across the crack, the rest of the Imperial Army arrived, their eyes wide as they realized what she had done.

Hearing the pounding footsteps of dozens of men, Mulan turned to see another group of invaders rushing at her from the opposite direction. She lifted her sword. But before the Rourans reached her, they came to a skidding halt.

Dozens of pairs of eyes landed on her and then peered into the steamy crag beyond. She saw them take in the Imperial Army standing behind her, swords high.

And then they turned and ran.

In the space that followed, the only sound Mulan could hear was her own pounding heart. They had done it! *She* had done it! They had held off the northern invaders.

But her victory was short-lived. The Imperial soldiers had not even given a shout of joy before the shriek of a hawk pierced the air. Looking up, Mulan saw the witch circling faster and faster as she watched the invaders run like cowards. Mulan knew the witch was the real enemy. Reaching behind her back, Mulan grabbed her bow and notched an arrow. Taking aim, she let it fly.

The arrow soared through the air. Mulan held her breath and waited. As she watched, the hawk turned. For the briefest of moments, it seemed like Mulan's arrow would do its job. But just before the arrow hit her, the hawk transformed, splitting into hundreds of smaller birds.

They filled the air, blocking the sun as they hovered. Then, in one fell swoop, they moved in for the attack. Loud shrieks filled the air as the birds dove at the Imperial Army. The men ducked, trying to fight off the creatures. But the birds kept coming.

"Tortoise formation!" Commander Tung cried, his voice cutting through the shrieks of the birds and the men's screams.

As the soldiers gathered together, lifting their shields above their heads so they resembled the shell of a tortoise, Mulan scanned the horizon. Her eyes widened as she spotted movement on the ridge of the snow-covered mountain that dominated one end of the valley. Atop it, she noticed dozens of Rouran archers readying their bows. Her eyes grew wider as she saw a large trebuchet being moved into position. The wooden catapult would take out dozens of Imperial soldiers in a single shot. The sling could hold a huge rock or dozens of smaller ones. It was a powerful—and deadly—weapon.

The birds had been a diversion. The Imperial Army hadn't won. Not yet. There was a second wave being prepared—and it was about to attack. Trapped in the valley below, Commander Tung and his army wouldn't stand a chance.

Lifting her hand slightly, Mulan saw the mountain reflected back at her in the blade of the sword. She had an idea.

Using the distraction of the tortoise formation, she snuck out from under the cover of shields. She whistled loudly and a moment later, Black Wind raced up. Jumping onto his back, she turned him toward the ridge. As they galloped away from the other soldiers, Mulan reached down and grabbed an Imperial helmet. Then another, and another, and still more. Satisfied, she continued toward the ridge.

Her last success had been lucky. But she was going to need more than luck to pull off this plan.

EIGHTEEN

Hidden in a high crevice, Mulan looked down at the ridge where the Rouran army prepared their attack. As she watched, one of the men shouted orders, sending some soldiers toward the edge of the ridge with bows and arrows while others loaded a large, heavy boulder onto the trebuchet. Groaning with effort, the men moved it into position so that it was aimed at the valley—and the Imperial soldiers—below.

Taking a moment to make sure she was ready, Mulan looked in front of her. The helmets she had taken from the battlefield were lined up in a row. Black Wind was safely hidden. She was ready. Lifting her bow, she turned and took aim at the Rourans.

Her first arrow flew through the air. There was a surprised cry as an invader fell to the ground. Then another. And another. It didn't take long for the soldiers to notice what was happening. One turned, and Mulan saw him scan the ridge where she was hiding. Spotting the Imperial helmets, he let out an angry cry. Shouting new orders, he had his men turn their attention from the valley. The trebuchet was moved until it, too, was pointed toward the mountain where Mulan stood, hidden from view.

At the leader's signal, the Rourans fired arrows at the row of Imperial helmets, unaware that they were nothing but empty shells, dummies to trick the enemy. When it appeared that the Imperial soldiers were unharmed, the Rourans grew angrier. Their attention turned to the trebuchet. Mulan watched and waited, hoping she had planned correctly.

A moment later, the group of invaders lit the fuel-covered boulder that sat in its perch on the trebuchet. Instantly, the boulder ignited, bursting into flame. The invaders released the trebuchet.

As the flaming boulder flew, Mulan held her breath. The rock was huge and heavy, and even though it had been propelled with great force, it seemed to move in slow motion across the sky. For Mulan's plan to work, she needed the boulder to fly strong and true.

Closer and closer the boulder flew until, with a loud boom, it slammed into the snowy mountain-side behind her. The noise of the impact echoed down the mountain and over the valley floor below. The Imperial Army, appearing as small as ants from Mulan's perch high above, seemed to pause as the sound reached them. Mulan waited, listening. She reached down and put her hand to the ground.

She felt it. Just the smallest of vibrations, but it was enough to tell her that her plan had worked.

Not waiting to see the result of the avalanche that had already begun to roll from its peak, Mulan took off running. She tripped and slid down the hard-packed snow, the ground shaking more violently as the avalanche became stronger.

Mulan heard the invaders' shouts as the rumbling grew louder, and then the shouts turned to terrified screams as behind her a wall of white appeared. It barreled toward them, unmindful of which army it destroyed in its path. The snow, long still, was now a freed beast, eating anything in its way. Feeling the wind from the avalanche behind her, Mulan picked up speed. But the snow kept coming. She whistled loudly, and Black Wind appeared. He raced to her side, and just before the snow engulfed her, she leapt onto the horse's back.

Together, they galloped ahead of the avalanche as it nipped at Black Wind's hooves. Behind her, the invading army was not as lucky. Without horses, and weighed down by armor, they disappeared into the wall of white.

Mulan didn't spare them a thought. She just kept riding, worry and fear growing in her stomach. When she had thought of her plan, she had forgotten one vital part: that she couldn't control the snow. She had wanted the avalanche to take out the enemy, and it had, but she hadn't thought through what would happen after that. Now the snow was heading straight toward the Imperial Army. And it wasn't slowing down.

Urging Black Wind on, Mulan saw the faces of the Imperial soldiers grow clearer as she made her way farther down the mountainside. She watched in horror as the runaway trebuchet tumbled down, end over end, before landing with a crash—right on top of Cricket. Her scream caught in her throat as she watched Honghui race over and push the trebuchet off his friend. Shoving Cricket to safety, Honghui got to his feet only to be hit with a wave of snow that sucked him down.

Mulan didn't hesitate. Slamming her legs against Black Wind's sides and yanking on the reins, she turned the protesting horse in the direction of the snow. As he struggled to move toward where Honghui had disappeared, Black Wind snorted with the effort. He could barely stay atop the snow, and on his back, Mulan struggled to remain atop him.

Suddenly, Mulan spotted Honghui's arm reaching up through the snow. Extending her arm, she managed to grasp his hand in hers and then, with the last of her strength, she pulled him onto Black Wind's back. He lay limp in the saddle, his eyes closed and his breathing shallow. Turning Black Wind once more, Mulan galloped ahead. As the land leveled out, the rushing snow began to slow, then stopped altogether.

The avalanche had ended.

In the silence that followed, Mulan brought Black Wind to a halt. Beneath her, the horse's sides heaved as he struggled to catch his breath. He had saved her—and Honghui. Reaching down, she gave him a grateful pat on the neck. Then she slid down to the ground.

With effort, she managed to get Honghui's unconscious body off the horse. Laying him down gently, she looked at him for a long moment, watching as his chest rose and fell. He was alive. At least she had saved him.

Hearing shouts from the other men who were coming free from their shock, Mulan gave Honghui one last lingering look. She wanted to stay to make sure he was really going to be okay, but she needed to make sure that was the end of the Rouran attacks. Turning, she disappeared into the fog.

Honghui's whole body hurt. Opening his eyes, he saw that he was lying near the rest of the Imperial Army. His head pounded, and when he went to stand, his legs nearly gave out from under him. The last thing he remembered was getting Cricket to safety. Then there had been a curtain of white. The next thing he knew, he was waking up on the ground.

But at least he had woken up. He had the oddest feeling, almost a memory tugging at him, that someone had helped him, though he knew that was impossible. Only the craziest of people would have run into the avalanche. Shaking off the thought, he made his way over to Commander Tung. As he approached, he heard Cricket calling out.

"Has anyone seen Hua Jun?" Cricket asked, his eyes scanning the area.

Hearing Cricket's worried question, Honghui saw Commander Tung take notice as well. His battle-weary eyes searched the men. Spotting Honghui instead, he called him over. "Have you seen Hua Jun?" Commander Tung asked.

Honghui shook his head, a pit growing in his

stomach. Had Hua Jun been swallowed by the snow? Or lost to an invader's arrow before the avalanche had even begun?

One of the soldiers gave a shout. Turning, Honghui spotted a figure silhouetted in the distance. The fog made it hard to make out the details, but as the figure came closer, Honghui inhaled sharply. It was the woman warrior he had seen in battle. There was no doubt about it. Her long hair flowed out behind her as she rode across the valley atop her giant horse.

"Black Wind?"

Hearing Cricket, Honghui turned, startled, to find the young soldier now right next to him. He was staring at the warrior as well. *Black Wind?* Honghui repeated silently. What was Cricket talking about? Black Wind was Hua Jun's horse. His mouth dropped open as the rider burst free from the snowy mist and fog right in front of them. The horse she rode *was* Black Wind. But if the horse was Black Wind, that meant the woman riding him was . . .

"Hua Jun?" Commander Tung said, putting voice to Honghui's thoughts.

The female warrior shook her head as she

dismounted her horse. "I am Hua Mulan," she said, her voice strong, steady—and feminine.

Honghui's head snapped back and forth between Commander Tung and the soldier he had known as Hua Jun. The commander's face grew pale and the slightest of tremors shook his hand as he stared at Mulan. Honghui could see—and understand—the struggle Commander Tung was under as he grappled with what was happening.

Mulan saw it, too. She straightened up, keeping her expression stoic. But Honghui saw the unease creeping into her body. Her shoulders fell just slightly; her hand quivered briefly. The proud warrior she had been was beginning to fade under the horrified gaze of Commander Tung.

Beside Honghui, Cricket gasped as he made the connection. "He's a *girl* . . . ?" Cricket said, shaking his head. The other soldiers mumbled and muttered under their breath as well, shocked by what they were seeing and hard-pressed to believe it. Honghui listened, his rage building. Hua Jun had lied to him. He, or rather *she*, had been able to tell him what to say to a woman not because she had spoken to one, but because she *was* one! He had allowed himself to be vulnerable in front of her, and she had even beaten him in battle—more than once. His cheeks grew red as he remembered the lake.

Meanwhile, Commander Tung's expression had grown icy. "You are an imposter," he hissed, his voice heavy with disappointment. "You have betrayed your regiment." Mulan hung her head in shame. Commander Tung went on. "You have brought disgrace to the Hua family."

His words cut Mulan like a sword through her heart. Her head flew up. There was nothing worse he could say. "Commander . . ." she begged.

The commander didn't let her finish. "Your deceit is my shame," he went on. "When we return to the capital, I will yield my command."

A shocked murmur moved through the soldiers. Resignation? That was nearly unheard of! Commander Tung's career spanned decades. He was one of the most powerful and well-known commanders in all the Imperial Army. Yet he would turn his back on it because of Mulan's deception? The men looked back and forth between the pair. Mulan may have helped them defeat the Rourans in this fight, but was the victory worth losing their leader? As the murmurs grew louder, Sergeant Qiang stepped forward.

"What is the punishment assigned to this imposter?" he asked.

Commander Tung didn't hesitate. "Expulsion."

At this, the murmurs grew louder, horror mixing with fear at the very word. Honghui saw Mulan shake her head. She took a step toward her commander, her eyes pleading with him to understand. "I would rather be executed," she said.

The commander ignored her, turning his back to her. Sergeant Qiang, stepping forward, took a deep breath, and as everyone listened, he formally sentenced her. "From this moment forward," he said, "you are expelled from the Emperor's Imperial Army."

As the sergeant's words slammed into Mulan, her body seemed to shrink into itself. Her eyes lost their light. Honghui watched, his emotions running rampant. Mulan deserved this. She had lied to them all, put every single one of them at risk. She had messed with his head—and his heart. But he still couldn't help thinking she had been recklessly brave to do what she had done. To walk among the army and risk exposure at every turn. But she had done it. And she had excelled at it. She had even saved them. *All* of them.

He shook his head, hardening his heart. It didn't matter. Not now. She had been expelled. She would spend the rest of her days alone and ashamed.

Mulan gathered Black Wind's reins and walked away, keeping her eyes on the ground, too ashamed to make eye contact with any of the soldiers. Honghui watched her go until she was just a speck on the horizon. Hua Jun, he realized as he turned and made his way over to his comrades, was no more. It was as it should be.

But if it was as it should be, Honghui wondered, why did it feel so wrong?

NINETEEN

Mulan felt hollow. She moved, but without direction or purpose. Over and over she heard the word *expulsion* and saw the look of disgust and disappointment on Commander Tung's face, the look of betrayal on Honghui's.

She had never meant to hurt them. She had just wanted to do her part. Yet somehow, all along, she had known this day would come. One way or another. But for one brief, happy moment, as she had caused that avalanche to wipe out the enemy, she had felt strong, proud. She had felt like she could do anything.

But for what? Now she was expelled. She couldn't retreat home. She couldn't return to the army. She had nowhere to go. So she just walked. She left the valley behind, heading up into the mountains with Black Wind by her side. With each step, the air grew colder, but she didn't notice.

Reaching the edge of a cliff, Mulan stopped. The whole of the world seemed to stretch out in front of her, the sinking sun setting the snow-covered ground aflame with reds and pinks. In front of her sat the Phoenix, its own feathers a bright complement to the scene. Mulan stared at the beautiful sight, and her heart broke still further.

Sinking to the ground, Mulan allowed herself to cry. The sobs wracked her body as she wrapped her arms around herself, seeking comfort she could not find. As her crying intensified, she struggled to catch her breath, her chest heaving and tight. She felt broken inside, like a part of her had been shattered and would never be made whole again.

"What have I done?" she said, looking over at

the Phoenix. "I can never face my family. . . . I can never go home. . . ." As she said the words out loud, a fresh wave of grief hit Mulan. She lowered her head. She was no longer the strong warrior she had become; she was a fragile, frightened girl.

As she sat there, she heard the Phoenix come closer. The bird wrapped one of her wings around Mulan. The comfort was too much for Mulan to take. The bird's unconditional love felt undeserved—but Mulan allowed herself to accept it, leaning into the Phoenix.

For a long moment, bird and girl were still as Mulan's crying softened. Just as she managed to get her breathing back under control, a shadow fell over them. Mulan looked up, and her eyes narrowed as she saw a group of black birds flying in formation. They swooped and lifted on the air currents in a beautiful—but sinister—dance.

There was something familiar about the birds. As Mulan followed their movements, she realized why. They were the same black birds that had attacked the army earlier.

As if on cue, the birds flew straight down at her, and as they did, they transformed. Now in place of the flock was the witch standing before them. Mulan and the Phoenix shared a look. At the bird's encouraging nod, Mulan pushed herself to her feet. Lifting her sword and summoning the little strength she had left, she met the witch's piercing gaze with one of her own.

"If you're here to kill me," she said, "I promise that won't be easy."

"Kill you?" Xianniang repeated, her eyebrows raising in surprise. She shook her head. "No. Your disgrace is worse than death."

The words were like a slap to Mulan's face. She tightened her grip on her sword, forcing herself to keep her breathing even and her expression calm. She didn't want to give the witch the satisfaction of seeing her pain. But she failed.

As the witch recognized Mulan's agony, her expression softened. "I understand," she said. She paused. Her eyes grew thoughtful, as though she were lost in a memory. "I was a girl like you when my people turned on me."

In her hand, Mulan's sword trembled. There was heartbreak in the witch's words. And for the first time since she had encountered Xianniang, Mulan saw her not as a witch, but as a woman. She had been quick to assume Xianniang was a terrible person because she had aligned herself with the Shadow Warriors. But Mulan had not stopped to wonder why. Why would someone with so much power submit to Böri Khan's command? But here it was: Xianniang's own people had shunned her. Looking at the witch, Mulan realized they had more in common than she could have ever known.

As if reading Mulan's thoughts, the witch went on. The pain in her voice was mirrored on her face as she spoke. "I've lived a life of exile. No country. No village. No family." Pausing, Xianniang made sure Mulan was looking at her as she added, "We are the same."

"We're not," Mulan said, even though the exact thought had just crossed her mind. "We can't be."

Xianniang shook her head. "We are. The more power I showed, the more I was crushed. Just like you. You saved them today—and still, they turned on you."

Mulan felt like the ground beneath her feet had grown unsteady. What Xianniang said was true. Commander Tung and the others, they *had* turned on her, despite everything she had done for them.

"Merge your path with mine," the witch said,

watching as Mulan wrestled with her thoughts. "We will be stronger together."

For a long moment, Mulan said nothing. She could not deny that, together, they would be a powerful pair. But what would she be sacrificing to turn her back on the world she knew? Slowly, the shaky feeling began to fade. "You follow a coward—a leader who runs from battle," she said.

Xianniang laughed. "Böri Khan did not run from battle!" she said. "That *coward* will take the Imperial City. And your emperor will fall."

The witch's words finally snapped Mulan out of her fog. *Fall?* she thought. What was the witch saying?

"That can't happen!" Mulan cried, strength once again flooding through her. She took a step forward.

"But it happens now," Xianniang said. Though she was using the words to goad Mulan, there was pain in her voice as she spoke, as if she didn't want them to be true. She took a step forward. "Join me. We will take our place together."

Mulan stared at the witch, her mind racing. Böri Khan had disappeared. He had raced away, and his army had been defeated . . . hadn't it?

Suddenly, Mulan understood what the witch was saying. Böri Khan wasn't defeated. Leaving the others to fall had been part of his greater plan. His disappearance was not a retreat. He was going to go after the Emperor himself!

Shaking her head, Mulan met the witch's gaze. She lifted her chin, transforming back into the same confident warrior who had defeated the Rourans on the battlefield only hours before. "I know my place!" she said. "It is my duty to fight for the kingdom and protect the Emperor!" Then she turned and let out a piercing whistle. As Black Wind raced over, she leapt onto his back. The sadness and despair she had been feeling only a short time before was replaced with a wave of determination and anger. Anger at the thought that Böri Khan might succeed. Anger that the witch's words had, for the smallest of moments, intrigued her.

Yanking on Black Wind's reins, Mulan looked one more time at the witch. Xianniang stared back at her, disappointment in her eyes. But there was something else there, too. Something that almost looked like admiration.

Without another word, Mulan began to ride back down the mountain. The Phoenix let out a loud cry and flew into the air, following her.

"They will not listen to you!" she heard Xianniang call to her. "It will always be a man's army!"

But Mulan didn't look back. Let Xianniang believe Mulan would never find a place in the Imperial Army. Mulan didn't care. All that mattered now was saving the Emperor. And to do that, she needed to warn Commander Tung.

"What is the meaning of this?"

Sergeant Qiang's voice boomed out over the camp as Mulan raced into the middle of the gathered soldiers. Ignoring the sergeant's question and the curious looks of the men, she leapt off Black Wind and ran over to Commander Tung. But seeing his stern expression, Mulan slowed her steps. When she reached him, she bowed low. Then, looking up, she forced herself to meet his eyes. "Commander Tung," she began. "We must ride to the Emperor! His life is in danger!"

Doubtful murmurs broke out across the camp.

The soldiers didn't believe her. Neither, it seemed, did Commander Tung. "Böri Khan's army has just been decimated. The Emperor's life has never been safer."

Mulan shook her head. "That's what Böri Khan *wants* you to believe. Please . . ." She stopped and looked around for support. Seeing nothing but cold stares, she went on. "You have to listen to me. . . ."

This time it was Commander Tung who shook his head. "Only a foolish man listens to someone whose very existence is a lie."

His words hurt worse than the witch's dagger. A part of her wanted to turn and slink away. But if she left now, everyone would be in danger. The kingdom's future was more important than her own pride. Taking a deep breath, she pressed on. "At the battle, Böri Khan rode off with a small fighting force. At first, I thought he was a coward in retreat, but now I realize he was heading east towards the Imperial City." She paused to catch her breath before plunging ahead. "This was his plan all along. While the army is focused on his attacks to the Silk Road, Böri Khan sneaks into the capital to kill the Emperor!"

She stopped. Her words hung in the air. She saw the soldiers shift on their feet as they processed her news. A few nodded their heads, realizing that what Mulan suggested made strategical sense. If the Emperor thought he was safe, he would be an easy target. Mulan turned back to Commander Tung. She saw the struggle on his face as he balanced his feelings of betrayal and his experience as a commander. Mulan knew that the commander saw the truth in her words. She just had to get him to look beyond her own lie.

"There is not an army in the world powerful enough to topple the Imperial City," Mulan went on, her words respectful but direct. "But perhaps a small, well-trained force could. When employed correctly, four ounces can move a thousand pounds."

Commander Tung paused. He looked at Mulan and she could see him softening ever so slightly. She had not just been a soldier. She had proven herself time and time again. She had been a perceptive student, a willing conscript, and a brave warrior. He *had* to see that. He *had* to see past her single mistake—no matter how big it was.

"You would believe Hua Jun!" a voice called out,

shattering the silence. "Why do you not believe Hua Mulan?"

Mulan's head whipped around. Her eyes scanned the crowd of soldiers watching her and Commander Tung. To her surprise, she saw that the voice of support belonged to Honghui. Looking right at her, he nodded, and she could have sworn she saw a glimmer in his eye. Although it was the smallest of gestures, it was huge to Mulan.

"She risked everything by revealing her true identity," Honghui went on, his voice growing stronger. "She is braver than any man here." He stopped and turned to the other soldiers, daring them to defy him. Daring them to disagree.

Watching him, Mulan pushed down the lump that was forming in her throat. Despite her betrayal, Honghui was standing up for her. It was more than she could have hoped for, and the wave of gratitude that washed over her was immense. But it only grew as the other soldiers, following Honghui's lead, began one by one to come to her defense. "I believe Hua Mulan!" one said. "Yes!" another added. Mulan's heart soared as Cricket, Po, and even Yao added their own voices to the growing chorus of support. They were standing by her; even without her disguise, they believed in her.

But did Commander Tung?

Mulan turned back to the leader. His face was unmoving, his expression impossible to read. For a long moment, they stood face to face, neither speaking, neither blinking as around them the soldiers' cries dimmed.

"Bring me my sword," Commander Tung said. As Sergeant Qiang moved to do so, the gathered soldiers exchanged nervous glances. What was the commander going to do? In front of him, Mulan braced herself, prepared for the worst. "Hua Mulan," Commander Tung began, addressing her by her real name for the first time. "Your actions have brought disgrace and dishonor to this regiment, to this kingdom, and to your own family." He stopped. When he spoke again, his voice was full of respect. "But your loyalty and your bravery are without question. You will lead us as we ride to the Imperial City." Turning, he addressed the other soldiers. "Ready the horses!"

As the men jumped into action, filling the valley with the sounds of swords, Mulan stood among her fellow soldiers. She had felt pride when she made it to the top of the shrine. And she had felt powerful when she had tricked the invading army and sent the avalanche careening down the mountainside. But none of that compared to what she felt now. She was going to save the Emperor. And not just as a soldier, but as a leader—and as herself.

TWENTY

The Imperial Palace was quiet. High in the sky, the sun cast long shadows across the throne room. Sitting on his throne, the Emperor was silent, lost in thought. He had heard more disturbing reports of Böri Khan and his Shadow Warriors wreaking havoc all along the Silk Road. It was only a matter of time before panic and fear spread through the kingdom. And with panic and fear came instability and danger.

This could not happen. He needed to protect his people and keep his kingdom safe.

Hearing the throne room doors opening, the Emperor looked up. His chancellor was coming toward him, urgency in his steps. When he reached the throne, he bowed low. Then, straightening, he spoke. "Your Majesty," he began. "A word in private?"

The Emperor nodded, trying to keep his face neutral as the other officials and attendants in the room moved away. He had known the Chancellor for a long time. For him to look this worried, something must be truly wrong.

Unfortunately, he was right. "Scouts have informed me that Böri Khan has infiltrated the city," the Chancellor said, his voice urgent. "He assembles at the New Palace with a small group of highly skilled assassins."

The Emperor bowed his head in thought for a moment, his mind racing at the news. Böri Khan was bold to go after the New Palace. The building, aptly named, was new and not yet finished. Built in honor of his father, it was important to the Emperor. It was also less guarded, which made it an easier target. If Böri Khan were to take it, it would also make for a good statement of his strength.

When the Emperor looked up, the kind expression he normally wore was gone. In its place was the expression of a fierce—and deadly—warrior. "Prepare my guards," he said. "We ride to the site immediately."

"Your Majesty," the Chancellor protested. "It is far too dangerous."

"Your loyalty and concern for my safety are greatly valued," the Emperor said. But it was clear he had no intention of listening to his advisor's protest. Motioning to the generals and other officials who had moved into the shadows to step forward, he prepared to give them orders.

But the Chancellor interrupted him before he could start. "If I may be so bold, Your Imperial Highness . . ." he began, earning him a stern look from the Emperor. But despite the look, the leader nodded for him to go on. "Put me in charge of your Imperial Army. At least allow me to have them follow you and surround the New Palace." The Emperor was silent as he weighed the Chancellor's words. Taking the silence as an opportunity, the

Chancellor pressed on. "Please consider your citizens. Your safety must be ensured."

The words struck the Emperor. While it was not what he would choose, the Chancellor was right. He was the Emperor. Throwing himself right into the enemy's waiting arms without backup was a foolish maneuver that could leave the Empire without a ruler. No, the Chancellor was right.

Turning, he gave his orders. "I am placing my chancellor in charge of the Imperial Guard. His command is my command." As the generals and officers bowed in assent, the Emperor went on, his voice loud. "This brute who attacks our trade routes! This murderer who threatens our way of life! I will kill this Böri Khan as I killed his own father. With my own hands."

Without another word, the Emperor strode out of the throne room. Behind him, the Chancellor watched. For several minutes, he stood there, his eyes narrowed and his hands clasped in front of him as all around the room, officials and generals fluttered about. After a few moments, he moved to one of the windows. A flicker of approval flashed in his eyes when he saw the Emperor riding away from the palace, flanked by his guard.

Turning, the Chancellor looked at one of the senior officers. "Assemble all Imperial Guardsmen immediately in this square. That includes every guard on every tower and every gate."

The announcement was met with shocked murmurs. "But who will protect the city?" the officer asked.

"You question the judgment of His Majesty the Emperor?" the Chancellor snapped, his words harsh.

Immediately, the senior officer shook his head. "Of course not, Chancellor," he said, backpedaling. "I will see to it immediately."

When at last the throne room was empty, the Chancellor walked toward the throne. As he did, he lifted his arm and pulled a pin from the back of his neck. As the man's body slumped to the floor, unconscious, a hundred small birds rose in his place. It had been Xianniang the whole time. The birds rose up and shot toward the open door. Soaring into the sky, they flew in a tight formation, shifting and twisting so they formed a long, dense shape.

They were a signal.

And down in the New Palace construction site,

Böri Khan saw it. A smile spread across his face. Xianniang had done it. She had convinced the Emperor to leave his palace open and unguarded and race right into his trap. The man was a fool. And now he would pay. Signaling to his Shadow Warriors, Böri Khan watched as they slipped into the scaffolding along the west watchtower and disappeared.

Mulan pulled Black Wind to a stop in front of the Imperial City gates. They had ridden hard from the Mountain Steppe Garrison, and the horses and their riders were tired. But spotting the gates open and unmanned, she and the other Imperial soldiers instantly went on the alert. Mulan's body tensed and she felt her skin prickle. Something was wrong. Spurring Black Wind on, she and her fellow soldiers raced into the city.

Citizens jumped out of the way in fear and surprise. The soldiers didn't slow until they reached the main square of the Imperial Palace.

As they entered the square, Mulan pulled back on Black Wind's reins. She slowed the horse and looked over her shoulder at Commander Tung. He met her gaze, her worry mirrored in his eyes. The square should not have been open. The gates shouldn't have been unprotected. Where were the men who were supposed to be guarding the Emperor and the palace?

There was the sound of creaking wood. Whipping her head around, Mulan saw the gates to the square shutting. A moment later, the doors slammed closed. They were trapped!

"Ambush!" Mulan shouted to the other soldiers as the nervous horses nickered and shifted on their feet.

Unsheathing his sword, Commander Tung yelled out orders to the soldiers, moving them into formation. Just as he finished, dark figures appeared on the balconies that ringed the square. A moment later, the figures shifted and came into focus, revealing themselves to be Böri Khan's Shadow Warriors. They leapt from the balconies, landing on the ground with dancer-like grace, their swords already raised for battle.

The commander turned to Mulan. "Protect the Emperor!" he ordered.

Mulan didn't hesitate. Jumping off Black Wind's back, she raced across the square. Her arms whipped her sword through the air in precise and fluid motions as she fended off the attackers. Behind her, Commander Tung called for the others to keep her path clear. Instantly, Honghui, Cricket, Po, and the rest of the soldiers ran ahead to fend off the warriors in Mulan's way.

Clear of her attackers, Mulan entered the palace in search of the Emperor. Quickly, she made her way to the throne room. As she ran, she silently thanked Commander Tung for his leadership and preparation. He had spent their journey to the capital describing the layout of the palace to her in case they were separated. She turned left and right and then went up a flight of stairs, reaching the doors to the throne room. Pushing them open, she walked inside. The outside noises of battle faded as the doors closed behind her. Spotting a figure on the throne, she hurried down the long room and then bowed.

"Your Majesty," she said, her racing heartbeat slowing when she saw the leader safe. "I am Hua Mulan from the Fifth Battalion. I've come to protect you."

"Impossible."

Mulan's head lifted in surprise when she heard the familiar female voice answer. Looking up, her eyes adjusting to the darkness of the room, she saw that it was not the Emperor sitting on the throne. It was Xianniang. The witch stared back at her. Then the woman stood up and spoke again, her voice laced with disbelief. "A woman leading a man's army."

Mulan's eyes narrowed. The witch could think what she wanted. The truth was Commander Tung, Honghui, and all the other soldiers had accepted her. And they were counting on her now. "Where is the Emperor?" she said, unsheathing her sword and advancing toward the throne.

But her steps slowed as she came closer to Xianniang. Pain and grief were etched on the witch's face, making her sharp features oddly more beautiful. She looked vulnerable—and scared. Mulan felt the urge to ask her what had happened. But she didn't need to. She knew without words. Böri Khan's victory might be approaching, but Xianniang was alone. In so many ways.

"You were right," Mulan said, lowering her weapon. "We *are* the same."

Xianniang gave Mulan a small, sad smile. "With one difference: they accept you, and they'll never accept me." The witch's words were full of emotion, and as Mulan watched, a tear dropped down Xianniang's cheek.

Mulan's heart ached for the woman in front of her. She had, only a short time ago, felt there was no place for her, either. Yet, ironically, it had been Xianniang who had given her strength to embrace her true identity. If only now she could make Xianniang see there was another way.

"All along, you told me my journey was impossible," Mulan said, softening her voice as she approached the throne. "Yet here I stand, proof there is a place for people like us."

"No," Xianniang replied, shaking her head, then bowing it in defeat. "It's too late for me."

Mulan sheathed her sword. She came to a stop in front of the throne, unarmed and vulnerable.

For a long moment, warrior and witch watched each other. Mulan didn't move, her breathing steady as she watched Xianniang struggle to pick a side. "Please," Mulan said, breaking the silence. "I need your help." Her voice, strong and proud, bounced off the walls of the throne room.

Mulan could not read the witch's expression. Then Xianniang took a deliberate step forward. Mulan's breath hitched. What was she going to do?

In answer, Xianniang let out a piercing shriek. Mulan's hands went to her ears as she watched the witch drop her dagger and run down the throne stairs—straight toward her. Just before she slammed into Mulan, Xianniang let out another cry and transformed into a hawk. Flying up and over Mulan's head, the witch disappeared through the doors at the end of the room.

Racing after her, Mulan burst into the hall and followed the hawk as it flew down the palace steps and out into the air above the Imperial Square. Her head arched back, Mulan tracked the bird as it continued out over the city and then turned, flying in the direction of the New Palace.

Mulan gave chase. Below her, Commander Tung and his men fought, pushing back the Shadow Warriors. Mulan clambered up onto a roof above the square. Her eyes locked on the hawk as she ran over the tiles. When she reached the end of one roof, she leapt onto another, making her way out of the palace and onto the tops of the nearby houses. Her steps were confident despite the uneven surfaces and the buildings' great height. In no time, she reached the construction site of the New Palace.

Only then did she slow. Leaping down onto the ground, Mulan stood catching her breath as the hawk swooped into the west watchtower. The faintest of smiles tugged at her lips. In her gut, she knew. Xianniang had answered her call for help. Somewhere amid the construction was the Emperor—and Böri Khan. Now Mulan just needed to find them.

"Why are you here?"

Böri Khan's voice boomed with anger as Xianniang flew through the window of the tower. Scaffolding covered the inside of the unfinished building. The Rouran leader stood on one of the raised wooden platforms, the Emperor tied to a pole behind him. Transforming back into her human form, she approached the Rouran warrior, ignoring the daggers he shot at her with his eyes.

The Rouran leader had no power over her anymore.

"The attack has met fierce resistance," Xianniang said.

Böri Khan's eyes widened in disbelief. "From who?" he snapped.

Xianniang almost smiled, but she kept her expression stoic as she responded, "A young woman from a small village."

Böri Khan laughed. "A girl?"

Walking toward the edge of the tower, Xianniang looked out over the construction site. On the ground below, she could see Mulan racing toward the tower. She was calm, composed, her face a study in focus. Turning back to Böri Khan, Xianniang shook her head. "No," she said. "A *woman*. A warrior." Her voice was strong and proud. "She leads a band of brave and loyal soldiers. The army is not far behind." She smiled as she saw her words make Böri Khan's face contort in rage. He looked out the unfinished window of the tower as if he might actually see the army. Instead, he saw Mulan making her way toward them—the warrior who threatened to ruin his plans.

"A *woman leads their army*," Xianniang

continued, each word slow and deliberate. "And she is no *scorned* dog."

"You led her here," Böri Khan accused, turning back to Xianniang. He sounded surprised.

"You shouldn't have trusted me," she said. The moment was an echo of their earlier conversation. Only now it was she who held the upper hand. Because she no longer needed him. And he knew it.

Böri Khan's face grew red and his hands, hanging by his sides, shook as rage enveloped him. He reached behind his back and grabbed his bow, notching an arrow and aiming it right at the witch.

Xianniang didn't move except to lift one perfectly arched brow. "What makes you think you can kill me?" she asked.

"I can't," Böri Khan replied. Fast as lightning, he turned and aimed the arrow away from Xianniang—and toward Mulan, who had made her way inside the New Palace gates and stood on the ground below. "But I can kill *her*," he said, letting the arrow fly.

Xianniang watched the arrow move through the air as if in slow motion. Looking down at Mulan, Xianniang knew she could not let the girl die at the hands of Böri Khan. The Rouran warrior had been the last in a long line of people who had made Xianniang feel trapped, afraid to embrace the power within herself.

Xianniang had been right. They were alike. Mulan had hidden who she was, perhaps not in the form of a bird, but under the armor of a man. Yet she had ultimately embraced who she was and allowed others to see her true self. Mulan had done what Xianniang could never do: she had become free. If Mulan were to die now, everything she stood for, all that she had fought for, would be for naught.

Xianniang knew what she had to do.

Leaping into the air, Xianniang transformed into a hawk. With a flap of her wings, she put herself right in the path of the arrow.

The arrow slammed into her body, knocking her out of the scaffolding. Wind whistled in her ears as Xianniang felt herself fall. Just before she hit the earth, Mulan's arms reached out and caught her. As Mulan lowered her to the ground, Xianniang transformed back into her human form. She looked up at Mulan and gave her a weak smile as she felt the life draining from her body.

Her head grew heavy, and Xianniang let it fall back. As she did so, she met Mulan's eyes, which were full of surprise and compassion. "Take your place, Hua Mulan," she whispered. And then, with one last breath, her chest grew still.

TWENTY-ONE

Mulan stared down at the woman in front of her. In death, the witch's face looked peaceful. The thought brought some comfort to Mulan. Xianniang had been many things, but she had, at her heart, been a strong warrior. She shouldn't have had to die. She shouldn't have had to suffer at the hands of Böri Khan for so long, just so she could feel accepted. But now, at least, she was free.

Getting to her feet, Mulan pushed away the

surprising grief she felt. The best thing she could do for Xianniang's memory now was defeat Böri Khan and save the Emperor. Grabbing her sword, she raced through the maze of construction. Shafts of light pierced the shadows and the wind blew through the beams and rubble, making a low hissing sound.

Mulan spotted Böri Khan. The warrior's back was to her. He stood in front of a large open furnace. Inside, molten metal flowed into a huge tub, filling it with red-hot liquid. Focused on the furnace, he didn't hear Mulan as she approached. Taking advantage of his distraction, Mulan scanned the area, looking for any sign of the Emperor. Her eyes traveled upward and stopped as she spotted him. He was tied to a pole and bleeding from several wounds, but he was alive.

Taking a deep breath, Mulan tiptoed over to a low beam and hopped on. Then she climbed, using the crossbars that zigzagged over the room to get closer and closer to the Emperor. She was almost to him when a large shadow loomed over her.

Böri Khan was in front of her, blocking her way to the Emperor. In the shadowy light, he looked larger than life, like something out of a nightmare. His gaze trailed over her body and she saw him sneer. "The *girl* who has come to save the dynasty," he said, his voice dripping with disdain.

Mulan knew that to Böri Khan she appeared nothing more than a young woman. But he was wrong. She was *much* more. Dropping into the warrior's pose, she lifted her sword. "If you surrender," she began, "I will assure you that your death is swift and painless."

In response, Böri Khan laughed. And then—he attacked. In a smooth, powerful stroke, he swung his sword down at Mulan. The move was so quick Mulan barely had time to lift her own sword to block it. But the movement knocked her off-balance, and she fell. With a thud, she slammed into a beam below her, the impact knocking the wind from her lungs.

As she struggled to her feet, Böri Khan came after her. She scrambled backward, jumping out of the way just in time to avoid his swinging sword. Creeping along the beam, she switched her gaze back and forth between Böri Khan and the Emperor.

Böri Khan kept coming, his cruel laughter bouncing off the beams. His sword whipped through the air, and Mulan somersaulted to another beam to stay out of the way. The metal clanged as his sword struck the beam where she had been just moments before. Taking advantage of the miss, Mulan raced upward, making her way to the Emperor. She heard Böri Khan roar with rage as he gave chase behind her.

Beam to beam they went, with Mulan barely staying ahead of the huge, hulking warrior. But stay ahead she did, and soon she had reached the captive Emperor. Turning just in time, Mulan met Böri Khan's sword as it once again swung toward her. The sound of metal on metal filled the air as she struggled to hold strong against Khan's onslaught. But then he swung one last time, and the motion was so powerful that it sent her sword flying out of her hand.

In horror, Mulan watched as the blade fell down, down, down toward the ground and then, with a hiss, dropped into the burning liquid of the furnace. Mulan let out a cry of despair as she watched her father's sword disappear, melting into nothing.

For a long moment, she stared at the furnace. She had lost her father's sword. She had lost everything. How could she stand a chance now against the great and powerful Böri Khan?

And then, from above, she heard a voice. "You are a mighty warrior."

Looking up, she met the Emperor's gaze. Even though he was trapped, he looked strong—and calm.

"Rise up like the Phoenix," the Emperor went on. "Fight for the kingdom and its people."

Rise up like the Phoenix. The Emperor's words hung over Mulan. Was this part of why the Phoenix had come to her? Had everything been leading to this moment? She thought back to the despair she had felt as she stood on the mountain cliff, exiled and alone. And then she thought about the strength she had found when she had faced Xianniang, and the power she had felt when she heard Commander Tung accept her. Despite the odds and the obstacles thrown her way, she had overcome. She *was* a phoenix. She had risen above it all and become a warrior.

Hearing the beating of wings behind her, Mulan slowly rose to her feet and turned. She gasped as she saw the Phoenix appear, wings spread. The bird was no longer the wretched creature she had been when Mulan first met her. She was beautiful. Strong. Magnificent. Her feathers nearly blinded Mulan with their vivid color.

Filled with a renewed sense of purpose and power from the Emperor's words and the Phoenix, Mulan turned to face Böri Khan once more. The Rouran warrior hesitated only a moment, surprised to see her resilience, and then he rushed at her.

Mulan raced to meet him. For a moment, it looked as if they were going to crash headfirst. But at the last moment, Mulan leapt. Soaring over Böri Khan, she landed on a thin bamboo pole behind him. Balancing perfectly despite the narrowness of the surface, she taunted Böri Khan with a smile.

The warrior roared and swung his sword, slicing through the bamboo. It split in half, but that didn't stop Mulan. Leaping to another, and then another, she jumped from pole to pole as Böri Khan continued to hack at the air wildly with his long sword. Reaching the end of the poles, she lifted her arm in the air as one of the pieces of cut bamboo flew into her outstretched hand.

Grabbing it, she jumped down to the ground and stood, the bamboo pole in front of her like a staff.

Her breath came in gasps. She was exhausted. Every muscle ached and even her bones felt sore. She had been fighting for so long. First to find her place in the army, then in actual battle against hundreds of fierce warriors—and now against the strongest Rouran warrior of all. She wasn't sure how much longer she could go on. But if she stopped, the Emperor would die, and what would become of the kingdom? Unbidden, an image of the tulou came to her. The peaceful village, full of the same families for generations. What would become of her home? Her family? She had to keep fighting. Taking a deep breath, she lifted the bamboo.

Once again, Böri Khan came at her. Using the staff, she blocked his sword and then spun, her movements fluid. The staff became a twirling blur as she moved this way and that. Böri Khan tried to follow the dizzying motion but he stumbled. Taking advantage of it, Mulan stopped spinning and whacked him across the face. He let out a cry as his hand went to his cheek.

Mulan kept moving. Racing back in the Emperor's direction, she heard Böri Khan on her heels. Turning around, she lifted her bamboo just as Böri Khan's sword sliced down toward her head. Mulan cried out as her bamboo spear cracked, breaking in two as the Rouran's sword met wood and then continued down, slashing a rope that hung nearby. Without the rope holding it steady, one of the giant crossbeams pressed against the scaffolding came free. It swung back and forth in the air above, between where Mulan stood and the Emperor was imprisoned.

Watching the long piece of wood, Mulan had an idea. She leapt for the crossbeam in an attempt to use it to get to the Emperor. But the beam was too high. Desperately, she grabbed at it and hung there, her arms wrapped around the beam in an awkward hug. With her added weight and the momentum of her jump, the beam began to tilt and spin.

Böri Khan, his face filled with rage, took a running leap and grabbed hold of the opposite end of the crossbeam. The wood groaned under their combined weights as they hung on either end. At the same time, Mulan and Böri Khan hoisted themselves to their feet on the beam. They swayed, their balance uneven as the beam beneath their feet rocked back and forth.

Peering down at the ground, which now seemed very far away, Mulan took a nervous breath. Böri Khan was not going to stop until he defeated her. She saw him begin to maneuver toward her, his weight causing the beam to raise up behind her, forcing her closer to the middle—and to the Rouran. It would only take one swing of his sword for Böri Khan to knock her off. She had every reason to retreat.

But then, as if there was something in the back of her mind that kept reminding her why she had to carry on, she heard Commander Tung's voice in her head, reading aloud the Pillars of Virtue. She heard the Emperor, urging her to rise like the Phoenix. She saw, in her mind's eye, the magnificent bird. And she knew, in that moment, she would not give up. Slowly, she bent her knees and lifted her arms, taking the now familiar stance of the warrior that the commander had taught her. With her center of gravity lowered, her balance grew stronger. The room around her faded and she was back beside the lake, practicing the moves

Commander Tung had drilled into the soldiers. As Böri Khan came at her, she moved forward and backward, pressing and then yielding, all the while staying steady and focused.

Böri Khan, on the other hand, grew less focused. As Mulan deftly met every one of his moves, his face grew redder. His sword's movements became less controlled. Letting out a furious scream, he lunged at her.

Mulan barely had to move. Using his energy against him, she let him race by on the narrow beam, grabbing the sword right out of his hand as he passed. When he stopped at the end of the beam, he turned, only to find the blade of his own weapon pointed at his throat.

As Böri Khan stared at her in surprise, Mulan leapt up, grabbing a rope that hung from the ceiling above. Then, using the Rouran's sword, she hacked at the rope holding up the crossbeam. Repeatedly she swung until, bit by bit, the rope began to fray. Then, with a loud creak, it ripped in two, sending the beam—and Böri Khan— plummeting to the ground below.

Not waiting to see if Böri Khan landed on

his feet, Mulan swung herself to the platform on which the Emperor still sat tied. Racing over, she furiously cut at his bindings. Mulan's heartbeat quickened as she desperately tried to free the Emperor. Hearing the man take a quick inhale, she turned and saw that Böri Khan was standing on the ground below, his bow in hand and an arrow aimed right at them.

Böri Khan pulled back the arrow.

Mulan cut faster.

As the Rouran let the arrow fly, Mulan cut away the final binding. The Emperor's hand came free, and just before the arrow could pierce his chest, he lifted his arm and grabbed it. With a look of defiance, the Emperor tossed the arrow into the air.

Both Böri Khan's and Mulan's mouths dropped open in surprise. But Mulan was quicker to recover. Watching the arrow arc up and then descend back toward the ground, she saw an opportunity. Leaping into the air, Mulan whipped her body around. Her foot came out and then, with a THWACK, she kicked the blunt end of the arrow. The movement sent it hurtling through the air—right toward Böri Khan.

Lifting his hand, the huge warrior tried to catch it. But he wasn't quick enough. Fueled with Mulan's power and strength, the arrow slammed into Böri Khan's chest, knocking him to the ground, where he lay, unmoving.

Silence descended as the reality of what she had just done filled Mulan. Her body shook with adrenaline and her knees grew weak. She turned. The Emperor stood staring at her with an expression she could not read. She immediately lowered her knees to the ground, bowing.

"Stand up, soldier," the Emperor said. Mulan rose. "Tell me your name."

Mulan took a deep breath, pausing for only a moment. She had just defeated Böri Khan, the most feared warrior in China. She had beat him with her own strength and skill and, in doing so, had saved the Emperor—and the entire kingdom. A warmth spread within her as she realized the magnitude of what she had done. Moments flashed in front of her: Xianniang sacrificing her own life. Commander Tung putting his faith in her. Honghui lifting his voice in support of her. She had spent so much time pretending to be someone she was not in the hopes of doing her part to help. And the irony was that all along, she had only needed to be herself. Lifting her head, Mulan met the Emperor's gaze.

"I am Hua Mulan," she answered, and as her name echoed through the tower, she smiled.

TWENTY-TWO

The Imperial Palace was aglow. Hundreds of colorful lanterns floated in the sky above as people filled the streets, their voices ringing with laughter and celebration. A parade, led by a large red dragon, made its way along the main street while music and the scent of food filled the air.

Mulan stood inside the throne room, her mind a blur.

The past few hours had been surreal. Immediately after telling the Emperor her name, fear had filled Mulan. While she had saved the Emperor, she had done so as a woman. And it was still illegal for her to fight as one. She had followed him from the New Palace to the Imperial Palace with a lump in her throat, convinced he was going to punish her. But to her surprise, he had brought her to the palace to honor her.

Now she stood in front of the throne, a tiny figure surrounded by dozens of candles that lit up the room, making it warm and bright. Behind her, the most important people of the city stood watching her intently. Among them were Commander Tung, Honghui, and the rest of her battalion. Even Ramtish and Skatch were there, both no worse for wear despite being forced into battle. In fact, they looked almost handsome, freshly washed and standing with pride.

Rising from his throne, the Emperor approached Mulan. She bowed and smiled when he encouraged her to stand once more.

"Hua Mulan," the Emperor began, his voice carrying over the crowd. "The people owe you a debt of thanks. I owe you my life. In gratitude for your service and dedication, I invite you to take your place among our greatest decorated warriors—as an officer in my Imperial Guard."

Behind her, she heard the surprised murmurs from the onlookers. What the Emperor offered was an incredible honor. In fact, it was the greatest honor any soldier could wish for. It took Mulan's breath away, and she had to move her gaze from the Emperor so he wouldn't see the emotion running over her face. Unfortunately, when she turned, she found herself looking right at Yao, who had tears of his own running down his cheeks as he watched Mulan with pride. Seeing the large soldier weeping made Mulan smile, and she turned back to the Emperor. She knew what she had to say.

"Your Majesty," she began, "I am deeply honored by this immeasurable invitation. But with humble apologies, I cannot accept it." Once more, the room filled with surprised mumbles as those gathered tried to make sense of her answer. Only Commander Tung seemed to understand, and he gave her a reassuring smile as she went on. "I left home under cover of darkness and betrayed my family's trust. I made choices I knew would risk their dishonor. Since then, I have pledged an oath to be loyal, brave, and true. In order to fulfill this oath, I must return home and make amends to my family."

There was a pause as the Emperor considered Mulan's words. Then he nodded. Raising his voice, he formally addressed the court. "Devotion to family is an essential virtue!" As his scribes took note of this new official declaration, the Emperor looked once more at Mulan. He did not say anything for a moment, his warm eyes seeming to peer into her soul. Then, as though satisfied with what he had seen there, the Emperor nodded again. This time, in a voice only she could hear, he said. "Very well, Hua Mulan."

Turning, he moved back to the throne. Dismissed, Mulan made her way toward the soldiers—her friends. The night was young, and the celebration was just beginning. For the next few hours, Mulan reasoned, she would forget her journey home and just enjoy life. She would have time to think about what to say when she saw her family—and her father—later.

Dawn was beginning to brighten the edge of the Imperial City as Mulan led Black Wind across a bridge toward the main gates. In the sky above a few lanterns drifted aimlessly, while a boat floated empty in the water below. The city was quiet in the post-celebration hour, as was Mulan.

"You can't leave."

Hearing Honghui's voice, Mulan turned, surprised by the emotion she felt as she looked over at the handsome young man. Throughout the night she had tried to find him, but to no avail. There was so much she wanted to say. She wanted to say how sorry she was and how she had wanted to tell him the truth all along. She wanted to say hello—and goodbye. But now that he was there, in front of her, she was at a loss for words.

Honghui walked closer, the rising sun making his hair light up and his eyes twinkle. He smiled as he approached, and Mulan couldn't help smiling back. "The Emperor gives his permission for me to leave," she said. "But you do not?"

"We've not said goodbye," Honghui answered.

"Goodbye, Honghui," she replied.

"Goodbye, Mulan."

There was an awkward beat as they stared into

each other's eyes, both clearly wanting—needing—
to say more, and yet neither wishing to be the first
to do so. Mulan shifted on her feet. Across from
her, Honghui ran a hand through his hair. Mulan
wondered what it would be like to take that hand
and hold it in her own.

As if reading her thoughts, Honghui did just
that. Reaching over, he tried to pull her hand free
from Black Wind's reins. Nervously, Mulan clung
tighter to the leather. Honghui shook his head.

"You still won't take my hand?" he asked. His
voice was soft, deep with emotion.

Why was she hesitating? Honghui was standing
there in front of her, asking for her hand, and yet
in that moment she was more frightened than
she had ever been—even more than when she had
faced down Böri Khan. This felt more real, more
dangerous, more important. The air was charged
with an electricity she could not yet define. Holding
in a breath, Mulan let her fingers curl around his.
As she did so, emotion flooded through her. She
gazed down at their fingers, now twined together,
and she saw a future. Lifting her eyes, she met
Honghui's gaze. For the first time she truly looked
at him and let him look at her . . . as Mulan. Her

head moved closer to his. Closer, and closer, until she paused, her lips inches from Honghui's.

"I've never kissed a man before," she said.

Honghui smiled. "Neither have I."

And then, Honghui brought his lips to hers. As they kissed, their fingers stayed locked and Mulan sank into Honghui. It was, she thought as a morning dove cooed somewhere nearby, everything she had hoped for and nothing she could have dared dream for. It was perfect.

Mulan reluctantly pulled back, breaking the kiss. Her cheeks flushed, she brushed a strand of hair out of her eyes and smiled nervously at Honghui. If she could have, she would have stayed there, on that bridge, kissing Honghui for the rest of her life. But she had told the Emperor she had amends to make, and she couldn't afford the distraction, no matter how pleasant it was.

Picking up the reins from where they had dropped, Mulan threw them over Black Wind's head. Then she jumped on the horse's back. With one last look, too afraid that if she spoke, her voice would break with emotion, Mulan turned and rode away. But before she had even reached the gate, she heard Honghui shout, "I will see you again, Hua Mulan!"

Turning, she saw him standing where she had left him, his hand in the air, waving goodbye. She smiled back at him. *Yes,* she thought, *I hope.* Then she urged Black Wind forward, disappearing through the gate and leaving the palace, and Honghui, behind.

After much traveling, Mulan finally rode into her village, her heart pounding. She had spent the entire ride from the palace thinking of what she would say when she was reunited with her family, but now that the moment was almost upon her, fear filled her. What if they didn't want her back? What if they were already disgraced? What if they told her to leave and never return?

As Black Wind's pace slowed, Mulan saw villagers begin to enter the courtyard, curious to see who had arrived. Spotting Mulan, their faces filled with interest. The Matchmaker stepped out onto her front steps, her angry face growing still angrier when she saw Mulan.

Stopping in the courtyard, Mulan saw the door to her home open. A moment later, her sister rushed out. Upon seeing Xiu, all her fear vanished. Jumping down, Mulan ran over to her sister and threw her arms around her. She was home.

Mulan pulled back. Looking at Xiu, she smiled warmly. The younger girl looked . . . different. But then her sister spoke, and her warm, happy voice was the same. "There is so much I have to ask you!" she said, grabbing Mulan's hand and squeezing it tightly.

Mulan laughed. "Tell me about you first," she said.

"I am matched," Xiu said, letting out her own laugh when she saw Mulan's surprised expression. "You will like him."

"I am happy for—" Mulan didn't get a chance to finish as her mother plowed between the daughters, throwing her arms around Mulan and embracing her. The older woman's arms shook, and Mulan let her mother cling to her. No words needed to be spoken. Mulan knew she had been forgiven.

But then, over her mother's shoulder, she saw her father. Zhou stood silently, leaning upon his cane. His expression was blank, his eyes impossible to read. Pulling free from her mother, she approached him. Once again, her heart began to pound nervously. She had practiced her speech to him a hundred times, yet still she struggled to find the words.

"Forgive me, Father. I stole your horse, I stole your armor . . . I stole your sword." She choked on the word. Stopping, she gathered the courage she had found on the battlefield and went on. "And I lost it—the sword is gone. I understand now how much that sword means to you."

Silence fell upon them as Mulan stared up at her father, desperate to hear his answer. And when he spoke, his voice shook with emotion. "It is my daughter that means everything to me." As tears dropped down Zhou's cheeks, he went on. "And it is I who owe you an apology. It was my foolish pride that drove you away."

Mulan began to shake her head but stopped as Zhou held up his hand. He looked at her, taking in the warrior clothing she wore and the way she carried herself, even when filled with emotion. He nodded slowly, as realization of who she was, who she had become, dawned. "One warrior knows another," he said, his voice now filled with pride. "You were always there, yet I see you for the first time." Reaching out, he pulled her into a hug. Mulan sank into it, feeling finally at peace.

As they stood there, Mulan's mother let out a happy cry and ran to thank the ancestors. Looking toward the shrine, Mulan smiled as she saw the phoenix statue, its head leaning, the wing crooked.

The moment was broken by a loud, nasally, and altogether unpleasant voice. Turning, Mulan saw the Matchmaker making her way over. "There is not a man in the entire kingdom who will marry Mulan now," she sneered.

Mulan was about to protest when her father stepped forward. He shook his head. "There is not a man in the entire kingdom who is good enough for Mulan," he said. Then he turned his back on the Matchmaker, and he and Mulan went and joined the rest of their family at the shrine. Reaching over, Mulan straightened the Phoenix's crooked head. "Thank you," she whispered. "Thank you for watching over me. Thank you for everything."

Suddenly, the sound of hoofbeats filled the air. A moment later, the Emperor's banner came into view, whipping in the wind as the Imperial Guard cantered into the courtyard. The villagers gasped as they realized who the men were. Their village had never been honored by the presence of the Imperial Guard—until now.

Mistaking their appearance for danger, Zhou turned frantically to his daughter. "Soldiers have come to punish you," he said. "You must hide!"

Mulan shook her head. "No more hiding," she said, walking over and waiting as the soldiers came to a stop. The leader removed his helmet. A smile broke over her face as she saw who it was. Commander Tung looked down at her and nodded. Then he turned to Mulan's father. "Hello, old friend," he said.

Still not sure what was going on, Zhou stepped in front of Mulan. "Tung Yong," he said, greeting the commander. "I am honored to receive you and the Emperor's Guard. But if you are here to discipline Mulan, you will have to get past me." His hand tightened around his cane and he stood up straighter. Only Mulan could see that his bad leg was shaking.

Commander Tung shook his head. "I do not believe that will be necessary." Looking over his shoulder, he signaled to one of the guards.

Dismounting, the guard took a long, ornate box from the back of his saddle and brought it over. Commander Tung raised his voice so that the entire village could hear. "Under order of His Imperial Majesty, the Emperor, I present this gift to Hua Mulan. She has brought honor to her ancestors, to her family, to her village, and to her country."

As the commander spoke, Zhou looked back and forth between his daughter and his old friend, struggling to process what was happening. All around them, the villagers watched with wide eyes, and the Matchmaker, who had been listening most intently of all, fainted dead away. Ignoring the sound of the woman falling to the ground, the soldier presented the box to Mulan.

Mulan looked down at the gift and then up at Commander Tung. She wasn't sure what to do. But at her commander's nod, she slowly opened the lid. She gasped. Inside was a sword. Mesmerized, Mulan lifted it from the box and pulled it free from its sheath. Holding it up, she twisted and turned it in the air, the edges catching the sun and making it shine. It was magnificent, and in her hand, it was graceful, too.

"As befits a great warrior," Commander Tung

went on, "the sword is marked with the Pillars of Virtue."

Zhou's eyes didn't leave his daughter's sword as he whispered the words he knew she would find there. "Loyal. Brave. True . . ." But as the sword moved, Zhou's voice trailed off. There was another character etched on the back of the shaft. "What is the fourth virtue I see?" he asked, confused.

Commander Tung smiled. "Read it aloud, Mulan," he said.

Slowly, Mulan ran a finger over the inscription. She read the word silently at first, and then aloud. "'Devotion to family,'" she said, the Emperor's decree now there as a permanent reminder of all that she had given in honor of her family.

Dragging her eyes from the sword, Mulan met her father's gaze. He looked back at her, overwhelmed with pride. As she watched, he straightened up, standing taller than he had even when he was in the army. Beside him, her mother and sister stood with pride in their eyes as well. "You have brought honor to us all," he said.

Mulan's breath hitched in her chest. It was all she had ever wanted to hear. It was the reason, she knew now, that she had fought so hard, and it had been what had made her find her chi and had driven her forward when she should have turned back.

Commander Tung's voice interrupted her thoughts, and she turned to look once more at the man who had helped her become a warrior. He looked back at her with pride. "The Emperor urges you to reconsider his invitation to join our greatest decorated warriors as an officer in the Imperial Guard." Once more, the villagers began to mutter, shocked to hear that their own Mulan had been offered such a glorious position. "He eagerly awaits your decision."

All eyes turned to Mulan, everyone curious to hear what she would say. From above came the sound of a powerful birdcall. It echoed over the tulou, causing everyone to crane their necks to see what could have made such a magnificent noise. Mulan smiled. She didn't need to look up to know what she would find there. But still, she lifted her head. There, in the sky above, was the Phoenix. Her outstretched wings flashed in a rainbow of colors as she dipped and dove on the wind. When Mulan saw the Phoenix, her smile grew broader. Her friend, her guardian, had come to check on her one last time. Satisfied with what she saw, the Phoenix let out another cry, and with a flap of her powerful wings, she soared away.

Watching the Phoenix go, Mulan whispered goodbye. She wasn't sure where her journey would take her. But she knew now that she had the strength to do anything. She was Hua Mulan, and she was a warrior.

THE END